The CRUISING SAILOR

Tom Dove

Editor: John P. O'Connor, Jr.

BRISTOL FASHION PUBLICATIONS
Enola, Pennsylvania

The Cruising Sailor by *Tom Dove*

Published by Bristol Fashion Publications

Copyright © 1999 by Tom Dove. All rights reserved.
No part of this book may be reproduced or used in any form or by any means-graphic, electronic, mechanical, including photocopying, recording, taping or information storage and retrieval systems-without written permission of the publisher.

BRISTOL FASHION PUBLICATIONS AND THE AUTHOR HAVE MADE EVERY EFFORT TO INSURE THE ACCURACY OF THE INFORMATION PROVIDED IN THIS BOOK BUT ASSUMES NO LIABILITY WHATSOEVER FOR SAID INFORMATION OR THE CONSEQUENCES OF USING THE INFORMATION PROVIDED IN THIS BOOK.

ISBN: 1-892216-15-9
LCCN: 99-072229

Contribution acknowledgments

Cover Design: John P. Kaufman. Photo by Tom Dove.
Inside Graphics: As noted.

The Cruising Sailor by Tom Dove

To Pam
My Mate, Shipmate and Compass

The Cruising Sailor by Tom Dove

The Cruising Sailor by Tom Dove

Introduction

Morning's pale watercolors play across the calm creek as I sip a mug of steaming tea and gently engage the world. My wife, Pam, runs on a slightly different clock than I; she will stir in another half hour. We anchored here last evening after a splendid, long spinnaker reach in a 12-knot breeze, whitecaps sparkling on the water as our boat slid effortlessly along, wake and wind the only sounds. It isn't always this perfect, but usually it is.

I've been escaping on sailboats for four decades. First as a break from studies, next as a cure for work pressure, then to vacation with the family, and now as a way of life. Although Pam had not sailed before we met, she added elegance to our cruising, to the benefit of the entire family. She became the Comfort Committee and her word was respected as law, superseding everything but immediate safety matters.

We've worked out many details for ourselves and have shamelessly stolen ideas from others until going cruising now is as simple and comfortable as staying home and a lot more fun. After 18 years with the same boat, we know every detail of its behavior. After living aboard for months at a time, we are truly comfortable afloat. After exploring the coast of the U.S. from New England to Florida, we still discover surprising things on every cruise.

Cruising in a sailboat is wonderful. It is also a splendid path to self-development, a lifetime sport for people of all physical abilities and a perfect environment for rearing children. In a complex world, cruising aboard your own boat may be the last refuge for living simply and well.

The aim of this book is to introduce newcomers to cruising under sail, although experienced sailors will find useful information and a bit of entertainment. I'll presume the reader already knows how to get underway in a simple boat, beat to windward, reach, run, tack and gybe.

Part of the attraction of sailing is the adventure of it, while part is the sheer pleasure of motion without effort. To keep the adventure at the proper level and reduce the effort of making the boat move, you need to know some things.

This book describes three different cruises, in fiction-based-on-fact stories, alternating with chapters about the technical details you need to choose a boat. I begin with a story of weekending in a small boat, because it is an axiom that small boats are best for learning, rewarding proper handling immediately and rebuking for errors with equal swiftness. The two succeeding tales raise the ante with increasing boat size.

This book is not about building your own boat or sailing around the world. It's about exploring the coast, perhaps with a short offshore jaunt thrown in from time to time. Many people think it sounds more glamorous to leap transatlantic to Ireland than to poke around the Chesapeake, harbor-hop along the Maine coast, or wander down the Intracoastal Waterway, but I respectfully disagree. Coastal cruising is more demanding (and to me, more rewarding) than ocean voyaging and most world cruisers see voyaging as a means to cruise a new coast. You can always add the skills you need to cross oceans to what you learn cruising coastwise, should that appeal to you.

Our vessels are officially classified as pleasure boats and that's what they should always be. With the right boat, the right equipment and the right information, you can travel in comfort and elegance as well as safety. Any size boat can be a yacht; it is attitude and preparation that makes it more than camping on the water.

As you cruise, you will become intimate with nature,

The Cruising Sailor by Tom Dove

fully experience places as no landlubber ever does and meet an amazing variety of fine people. Turn the page and begin *The Achievable Dream.*

Tom Dove

The Cruising Sailor by Tom Dove

The Cruising Sailor by Tom Dove

Table Of Contents

Introduction		Page 7
Chapter One	Talking About Boats *Size -- Length -- Beam Draft*	Page 15
Chapter Two	The Small Cruiser *Factual fiction*	Page 19
Chapter Three	Hulls & Rigs *Hull form -- Rigs*	Page 27
Chapter Four	The Mid-Size Cruiser *Factual fiction*	Page 39
Chapter Five	Talking About Boats *Weight -- Power -- Speed Stability -- Comfort Putting it all together*	Page 49
Chapter Six	The Full-Size Cruiser *Factual fiction*	Page 61
Chapter Seven	Arriving & Staying Put *Anchors -- Rodes -- Marinas*	Page 69

Chapter Eight	Soundness *Construction techniques Materials -- Surveys*	Page 79
Chapter Nine	The Cruising Spectrum *What to Expect*	Page 91
Appendix One	Boat Design Formulas	Page 95
Appendix Two	Sources	Page 97
Appendix Three	Tools & Supplies	Page 101
Glossary		Page 111
Index		Page 125
About The Author		ISBC

The Cruising Sailor by Tom Dove

The Cruising Sailor by Tom Dove

The Cruising Sailor by Tom Dove

Chapter 1
Talking About Boats

Every field has its specialized terminology. While the language of sailing seems complex at first, it is far simpler than, computers or gourmet cooking -- and more colorful, even when the sailor isn't swearing. Absorb the concepts and words and you'll be able to mingle with folks at any cruising get-together in the world.

Size

How big is a boat? That depends on how you measure it. The external dimensions are length, beam (width) and draft (depth), but there's more to it.

Length

Most builders identify their boat by the length overall (LOA), so you will see advertisements for a Beneteau 30, a Catalina 30, or a Hunter 30: all are approximately 30 feet LOA. One current marketing trend is to add zeroes, so a 32-footer becomes a "320" or a "3200," while other builders try to stand out from the crowd by adding a third digit to indicate fractions of a foot, making a 36.5 - foot craft a "365." A few use metric designations, like "105" for an LOA of 10.5 meters (just over 34 feet), while even in some fiercely metric countries like France, boat lengths are often given in feet.

The length on deck (LOD) is actually a more representative dimension and it may not be the same as the LOA. One 22-foot LOD boat has a six-foot bowsprit which makes its LOA 28 feet and another 32-foot LOD cruiser's anchor platform sticks out to make an LOA of 34 feet. That's rarely a problem, although marina slip rentals are often priced by the foot, based on the LOA.

In this book, I consider boats from 20-28 feet LOD to be small, those from 28-36 feet mid-sized and those from 36-45 feet large. Most vessels much larger than 45 feet are unwieldy for handling by one or two people, although there are some interesting exceptions. There's plenty of overlap among these three categories; new 28-footers often have as much space as older 32-footers and both should properly be called "mid-sized."

The best indication of interior space is the length on the waterline (LWL). Since the cabin floor space, the furniture and most of the stowage areas are near the waterline, the available room inside a 30-foot LWL boat will be significantly greater than in one with a 27-foot LWL, although both may be 35 feet LOA. The 30-foot LWL boat will also have a higher potential speed for reasons related to the physics of wave making. More on that later.

Beam

The stated beam is generally the maximum width (extreme beam) of the hull, although sometimes the waterline beam is listed as well. Not only is the overall beam important when you're trying to squeeze the boat into a narrow marina slip, but this number can tell you about its stability, interior space and sailing qualities, when taken together with the other principal dimensions.

A beamy boat will have much more interior space than a narrow vessel and modern designs have pushed beam to its limits. Part of this design trend is to carry the maximum beam well aft, almost to the stern, creating a large cockpit. Doing this also makes it possible to squeeze an aft cabin under the cockpit seats of boats as small as 28 feet LOA, but at the expense of stowage space for sails, fenders and lines.

A big, beamy cockpit creates problems of its own. Sailors under 5'6" should check carefully to see if they can brace their feet when the boat heels. My wife spent a bruising week on a friend's boat bouncing around the wide cockpit because there were no footrests to keep her from sliding off the seat.

Old, heavy displacement designs usually had small cockpits, often little more than foot wells. Traditional designers knew there was a danger of being "pooped" by breaking waves in storms offshore and a big cockpit could hold enough water to sink the boat. The current trend is toward large cockpits with huge drains, so any water that does come aboard sloshes back out just as fast. The hottest racing craft eliminate the transom entirely so waves can sweep the deck or the cockpit without causing permanent damage. It's uncomfortable to have your ankles in water whenever it's rough. It is best to develop your own preferences as you talk to sailors who have both kinds of boats and gain experience on a variety of vessels.

Draft

Draft, the distance from the waterline to the bottom of the keel, determines how deep the water must be to keep the boat afloat and that's important. One oysterman said of the Chesapeake Bay, "There's lots of water out there, but some of it's spread a mite thin." The same is true of the southeast coast of the U.S., the Bahamas and many other interesting cruising grounds. While deep draft boats usually have more storage space, greater ultimate stability and slightly better performance to windward than shoal draft (shallow) boats, coastal cruisers willingly trade some of those qualities for the ability to creep into cozy coves.

Not much is usually said about air draft, (overhead clearance), but it is as important as water draft where bridges are plentiful, such as in the Atlantic Intracoastal Waterway (ICW). I knew one man who traded up for larger and larger boats over the years, finally ending up with a big, beautiful vessel with a mast so tall he couldn't get under the fixed bridges that crossed his favorite rivers. When I last saw him, he had gone back to a 40-footer with a reasonable mast height. Think ahead when you consider water and air draft. Perhaps you are cruising Maine now, where the bridges are few and the water is deep, but what if you decide to go south for the winter one year?

Major waterways usually have bridge and overhead cable clearances of at least 55 feet, but there are exceptions; the St. Johns river and the Okeechobee Waterway in Florida are two scenic routes with limited overhead clearance. A tall mast will also keep you from enjoying the best sailing waters of Pamlico Sound in North Carolina.

One pretty cruise is up the Hudson river, through the New York State Barge Canal and into the Great Lakes; it's the famous Erie canal route of history and song. For canal cruising like this, you need a simple way to lower the mast to sneak under low bridges and such an arrangement makes mast and rigging maintenance easier, as well.

The Cruising Sailor by Tom Dove

Chapter 2
The Small Cruiser

Friday was the best day of the week and it got better by the hour.

Brian and Kate enjoyed their work, but after five days of computer screens and deadline crises for her, paper grading and lesson planning for him and protracted meetings for both of them, they needed to get away and recharge their batteries. In summer, that could mean camping, bicycling or hiking, but here in south Florida, winter meant sailing.

They had taken a class at a sailing school, mostly out of curiosity. Both quickly became addicted to the sensations of sail. After enjoying chartering a few times, with a professional crew on a large yacht and bareboating with another couple on a 36-footer, they realized they wanted to own a boat themselves. It had to be small and handy, yet large enough for overnighting or spending a weekend in "camp cruising" style. It had to be easy to maintain, stable and fun to sail. The price had to be low, so they would be able to use their income for other pursuits as well as sailing.

The big sailboat show at Annapolis in October was a chance to look at all the new boats in their size range and the magazines were full of articles and reviews, but they decided to start with a used boat. It made more sense to see how much they liked the sport before investing a large sum. They did start collecting brochures and reviews of new vessels that looked interesting, including the cards of brokers and dealers who had impressed them at the show. If they liked cruising, they would be back in a couple of years for their next boat, which might be a new one.

Each weekend, Brian and Kate took their collection of newspaper advertisements and went to look at boats, since brokers rarely listed the low-priced, entry-level vessels they sought. There was a wide range of choices; the popular Catalina 22, Venture/Macgregor 22 and 24, O'Day 22, Tanzer 22, Ensign and other small craft from the 1970s were contenders and they might have chosen any one of them, but a bargain came up on a 24-foot Rainbow that was too good to miss, so they bought it. For less than the cost of a week's charter, they were owners of a sturdy daysailer/overnighter and a trailer to carry it behind their pickup truck.

The Rainbow was designed by Sparkman and Stephens as a strong, low-maintenance rental and instructional boat with comfortable seating and an emphasis on safety. The client had said, "Give me a boat that will take six drunks out in a thunderstorm and bring them back," and that is what S&S did.

The rig was a masthead sloop with a reasonable amount of sail that could be increased with a larger genoa jib and a racing spinnaker. The hull was narrow by modern standards, with a relatively short waterline. The cockpit seats were deep and comfortable, the lazarette was spacious and the cuddy cabin had Vee berths that would sleep two cozily. A portable toilet was in the cabin, but privacy demanded installing a curtain over the little doorway. Power was a six-horsepower, long-shaft outboard motor which would drive the craft to its hull speed (about five knots) easily. Flotation under the seats insured ultimate safety in the event of swamping or punching a hole the hull and there was no exterior wood to require sanding and varnishing.

Spending a weekend on this boat was not luxurious, but they were accustomed to camping in a tent, so those skills transferred easily. They had made a number of small changes and additions during the previous two years. None was costly, but each increased the comfort, safety or convenience of the boat.

The first requirement was comfortable bunks, so they ordered thick foam cushions for the Vee berths, covered with a durable acrylic fabric. Instead of sheets and blankets, they bought a double sleeping bag with Summer and Winter sides of a different thickness; when a winter cold front moves through Florida, temperatures drop near freezing for a short time, no matter what the Chamber of Commerce says. High-quality, foam-filled pillows completed the sleeping arrangements. They wisely decided not to scrimp on sleeping comfort.

Cooking was next, although they would not prepare elaborate meals aboard. The boat's original single-burner, Sterno fired "Sea Swing" stove that came mounted in the tiny cuddy cabin didn't fit any of their camping cookware and they saw little reason to cook inside when the cockpit was so much more spacious. Gasoline was far too dangerous as a cooking fuel on a boat, as its explosive fumes would settle into the bilge and the portable stoves that used small bottles of propane also seemed risky as well as rust-prone. They finally chose a single-burner Origo stove that burned non-pressurized alcohol. This little gem made coffee as fast as their range at home and was very safe; even if they spilled some burning fuel, water would extinguish the flames. After experimenting with a variety of brands of alcohol, they realized that proper performance depended on using the highest quality fuel available. A gallon would last the entire season, so the higher cost of the good stuff was not a problem.

Brian was a penny pincher and he always looked for the cheapest solution to any problem, but Kate blunted his excess thriftiness whenever it seemed that quality was important. The bunks and bedding were one example, but she had also insisted on good binoculars and the best charts. He was happy with his inexpensive plastic navigation tools, battery-powered lights instead of a built-in electrical system, and surplus-store cockpit awning.

The Cruising Sailor by Tom Dove

WAVE DANCER was docked at a private pier on the Florida Bay side of Key Largo, less than an hour's drive south from their condo. The boat could have stored on the trailer in a marina, but that would mean putting it into the water with a crane or forklift each weekend, which was more expensive. That was one disadvantage to a keel boat. If they had bought a centerboard vessel, they could have launched it from the trailer at any public ramp, extending their cruising possibilities. The second drawback was the keel's fixed 3-1/2 - foot draft; when aground, they couldn't simply lift a centerboard and drift off the sandbar, but had to turn the boat, heel it over and sail it off.

But the keel had advantages. The Rainbow consistently out sailed the centerboarders, especially to windward, and it was very stable. The deeper ballast also made it feel like a big, substantial boat and they both liked that. As they shopped, they had come to know the truth of the statement, "Every boat's a compromise." This wouldn't be their ultimate boat, but for price and convenience, it suited them well now.

The weekend's preparations had actually begun on Thursday, when they cooked a fine stew in a Crock Pot during the day, then froze it in a plastic container. This would be Saturday night's dinner, serving as additional ice in the portable cooler until then. Friday night, they would dine at a little restaurant near the boat, then sleep aboard at the pier before departing the next morning. The two lunches were simple sandwich makings packed in plastic containers. They liked cereal and fruit for breakfast, so a couple of boxes of UHT milk also went into the cooler. Some weekends, they would fix a supper of omelets with strawberry preserves folded in and then flambéed in rum and served with a dollop of sour cream.

Limited storage space and lack of running water precluded using china and stemware aboard, but good paper plates, napkins and plastic cups, color-matched to the canvas of the boat, served well. Kate bought an attractive, matched set of utensils at a boat discount store and made other small but significant efforts to create a pleasant environment for dining.

The Cruising Sailor by Tom Dove

She wisely insisted that touches of elegance were essential to the cruising experience. They could have simply heated up cans of food or existed for two days on trail mix, but this was yachting, not survival training. It didn't matter that the boat was older than they or that it had cost less than a pop-up camping trailer; attitude was the key.

"The weather looks good. Ten to fifteen knots out of the southeast and no cold fronts in sight. Where should we go?" Brian asked as they stowed the awning and hung the outboard motor on the transom.

"Butternut Key is neat. Remember the little sharks there?" Kate said. "The mallards should be here for the winter by now and the roseate spoonbills are gorgeous."

"We could see some of those going through the Cowpens," he said. "How about trying that channel just off Snake Creek near Plantation Key?"

"Snake Creek. How romantic."

"You want romance? That can be arranged," he said with a gleam in his eye.

"Would that be a good, safe place to try out your new bathtub boat?"

"You're making fun of me again. That's a cost-effective, low-technology, inflatable craft."

"Looks like a cheap, flimsy, blowup plastic pool toy to me," she said.

They dropped the mooring lines, motored out into open water, headed up into the wind and raised the mainsail and jib. It was always a pleasure to shut off the motor and hear only the swish of wind and water. The feeling of motion without effort was wonderful.

A fast reaching course southwestward took them past tiny patches of mangroves and across gin-clear water where they could see coral heads six feet below. It was like flying at low altitude.

In early afternoon, they swung back into the wind, furled the sails and motored slowly into Snake Creek. The

The Cruising Sailor by Tom Dove

channel was uncertain and the side channel where they anchored even trickier, but their shallow draft and the clear water made for easy eyeball navigation past the coral heads and soon they dropped the anchor, set it and spread the awning over the big cockpit.

"This isn't as pretty for snorkeling as the Cowpens anchorage," Kate said.

"I'll blow up the dinghy and we can row over there tomorrow," Brian answered.

"You go first. I don't trust that thing," she said.

Darkness was falling fast as he pumped up the discount-store plastic boat, slid the short oars into their sockets and pushed the whole thing overboard.

"See? It floats," he said triumphantly. "Let's see how she rows."

"One small step for man," she answered. "Take the bag with the anchor and flashlight along."

He cast off the bow line and began rowing toward the bow of WAVE DANCER, into the wind which had steadily increased during the day and was now blowing 20 knots. After two or three hard pulls on the oars, one flimsy plastic oarlock broke. With only one oar, he could go only in circles and the wind quickly blew the little boat out toward Florida Bay.

By now it was very dark and Brian's situation was suddenly serious. No oars, no radio, no land to leeward for hundreds of miles and a wind that was building fast.

"Raise the anchor and come get me!" he shouted.

He felt a sudden, deep sadness as he realized that the disappearing anchor light on WAVE DANCER meant he might never be found.

Suddenly, he remembered the canvas bag Kate had tossed into the dinghy at the last moment. He pulled out the little anchor, secured the end to the sturdiest point he could find on the boat and dropped it over. After two bounces on the hard limestone bottom, it caught and held.

But he still might be stuck there until daylight unless

the flashlight worked.

It did.

WAVE DANCER was now invisible in the darkness, but he aimed his light at what he thought might be its anchor light, holding his breath out of anxiety and for steadiness.

Could his wife raise the anchor, start the engine and find him by herself? He was not confident of that, as she had never single-handed the boat before.

Was the anchor light moving? Yes! She had gotten underway.

In a few minutes, the dinghy was alongside WAVE DANCER and a deeply grateful husband was hugging a relieved wife.

"That's what you get for being a cheapskate," she said as they motored back to the creek.

"Yes, dear."

"Good thing I didn't buy cheap batteries for that flashlight," she continued.

"Yes, dear."

The humbled sailor opened the flashlight and recognized the brand as one that had run a series of ads about how their batteries had saved lives. Back at home the following week, he wrote the company a letter describing his adventure. They sent him a check for the story and made a television advertisement of it, changing the protagonist into a grizzled fisherman for stronger visual effect.

He used the money to buy a good dinghy.

The Cruising Sailor by Tom Dove

Chapter 3
Hulls & Rigs

The pointy end usually goes first, the mast goes up and the keel goes down. Beyond that, there's a world of variety in hulls and rigs.

Hull Form

Favored hull shapes change like dress fashions and what was popular in boats a decade ago is out of style today. That doesn't make the older boat undesirable; many sailors prefer the lines of earlier times.

Often, a racing rule will favor a particular type of boat or hull contour, so designers draw vessels that perform well under that rule. This has given us the long, thin Meter-class boats of the 1930s, the classic CCA yawls of the 1950s and the wide skimmers of the 1980s. Cruising boats are influenced by racing designs and as a result they have become lighter, faster and more fun to sail.

Eventually, a race-driven design fashion leads to disaster. Read about the Fastnet Race of 1979 or the losses of famous single-handed racers in the 1990s for examples of extreme design turning deadly. As cruisers, we don't need that last bit of speed to set a record, so we can enjoy healthier vessels.

Even cruising boat design is somewhat trendy. The cruising rage of the 1970s was the double-ended hull, usually with heavy displacement and a cutter rig for ocean voyaging. The 1990s gave us very long waterlines (sometimes with an LWL as long as the LOA) and wide, shallow hull forms. Each extreme has drawbacks. The heavy ocean cruising cutter is a dog to sail in the light breezes of coastal waters and many modern long, shallow hulls lack the capacity for food and other supplies that the crew needs for long-range sailing.

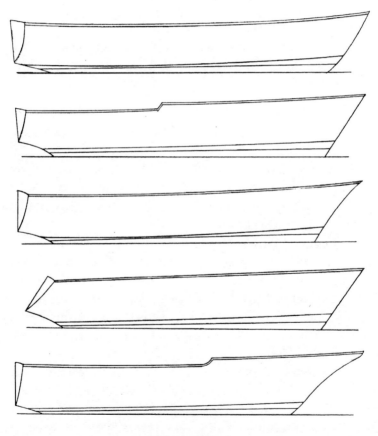

Arthur Edmunds
Figure 1

Currently popular hull shapes.

The Cruising Sailor by Tom Dove

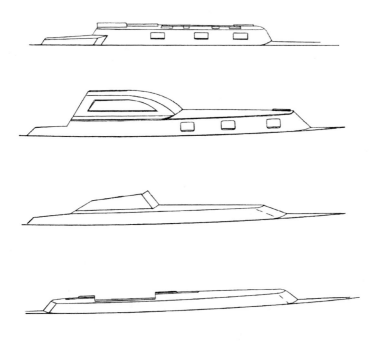

Arthur Edmunds
Figure 2

Currently popular topsides shapes.

A recent design trend is toward boats with high sides, or freeboard. While high freeboard produces a large interior with plenty of headroom, it also makes the vessel difficult to maneuver in strong cross-winds, especially if it also has a shallow keel or is lightweight. Such a craft will be blown sideways across the water like a chip of Styrofoam®. The typical planing powerboat, with high freeboard and small underwater area, illustrates the close-quarters handling problem; sit on the fuel dock of a marina on a weekend afternoon to see for yourself. In rough water, the waves may strike high sides hard enough to make the crew feel they are living in a bass drum.

Be moderate like Socrates and eschew the extreme designs of any era. Many production boats from the past and the present are wholesome, moderate vessels that make excellent cruisers.

Describing the exact contours of a hull and designing the rig that will power it are in the realm of the naval architect, not the amateur. Whatever type of boat you buy, get one that was drawn by a reputable designer.

While the underbody configuration is part of the hull and must be designed to match the other lines of the boat, keel and rudder development have been rapid in recent years, primarily as a spin-off of racing. The famous winged keel of AUSTRALIA II, which beat the 12-meter racing rule in 1983 and produced an exceptionally fast boat, was only one example.

Today, we have a wide range of underwater blade contours on cruising boats. Some skippers prefer the long keel with an attached rudder for shallow draft, resistance to snagging underwater objects and good directional stability. These qualities come at the expense of windward sailing performance, light air speed and maneuverability. Most choose fin keel boats with a separate spade rudder; they are faster and more fun to sail in light air and to windward but usually do not hold a straight course as well as a long-keeled boat.

John P. Kaufman
Figure 3

Full keel design with supported rudder.

The Cruising Sailor by Tom Dove

The wing keel enjoyed a brief spurt of popularity following the 1983 Cup races, but it has its own drawbacks. Run aground with a standard fin keel and you can move weight to one side to heel the boat over, reducing the draft and slip off the sandbar. Heel over a wing keel and the draft increases. You may be able to sail in shallower water with the wing keel, but it will be harder to rescue yourself it you do hit bottom. Those wings are also tempting targets for submerged lines and other obstructions.

Tom Dove
Figure 4

Fin keel design.

Tom Dove
Figure 5

Wing keel design.

A compromise design is currently popular. The bulb/fin keel, based on a design by Henry Scheel, gives shallow draft and good efficiency without the drawbacks of the wing keel. The bulb serves as an end plate to improve water flow as well as keeping the greatest weight down low where it is most effective. All bulb keels are not equal; the design is critical to efficiency.

Tom Dove
Figure 6

Modified bulb keel design.

Rigs

Sail arrangements are a source of endless discussion among sailors and such debates always seem to end up as statements of personal preference, not engineering fact. I like sloops (one mast, one jib, one mainsail), because they are simple and efficient. Part of my choice is familiarity; I've simply spent more time sailing sloops than other rigs and have worked out routines for handling the rig.

Many cruisers prefer the cutter (one mast, two jibs, one mainsail) because it allows a greater variety of sail combinations for different wind conditions and breaks up the area into

The Cruising Sailor by Tom Dove

smaller, more easily handled sections. You may leave the anchorage in an eight-knot breeze that calls for the big genoa jib, then it pipes up to 12-15 knots and you need to reduce sail. It's easier and more efficient to roll up the jib completely and unfurl the small jib, called a staysail, than to drop the genoa and replace it with a smaller sail, as you must do on a sloop.

On the down side, cutters are much more awkward to tack than sloops, as the outer jib can snag on the stay that supports the inner jib, or staysail. I have sailed a number of cutters and only one, equipped with sails made of a special slippery cloth, did not have this problem. The cutter rig is also more complex than a sloop, requiring an additional stay, a second roller furler, another halyard and set of sheets and perhaps even the nuisance of running backstays which must be reset each time you tack.

I suggest if your sailing will be on bays, sounds and rivers, the sloop's easy maneuverability will prevail. If you expect to spend most of your time crossing oceans or making long coastwise passages, the cutter's versatile sail plan makes more sense.

Larger boats do require larger sails and 400 square feet is about the maximum area one average sailor can handle. Dividing the rig becomes desirable when the sails get really large, perhaps to create a ketch (two masts, one or two jibs, one mainsail, one mizzen ahead of the rudder post) or a yawl (two masts, one or two jibs, one mainsail, one mizzen abaft the rudder post). Most of us are sentimental about the schooner (two or more masts, one or more jibs, one mainsail, one foresail, perhaps other sails on the extra masts); they are lovely but inefficient by modern standards. Schooners were popular along the East Coast of North America in the 19th century because they could be sailed by a smaller crew than a square rigger, required relatively short masts and rarely needed to sail to windward.

Sail handling gear has developed rapidly in recent years. Few cruising sailors still use jibs that are fastened onto the forestay with snaps or hanks; roller furlings are now reliable and nearly universally accepted. A properly designed set of lazyjacks from the mast to the boom can keep the mainsail under control while you raise or lower it and proprietary systems like the Dutchman® accomplish the same end.

Many builders today lead the halyards from the base of the mast back to the cockpit, but this is a mixed blessing. It would be handy to be able to raise and lower the mainsail without going out on deck, but the last few feet of sail always seem to bind someplace, requiring a trip forward, anyway. I suspect the driving force in these designs is marketing, not practicality. Cockpit-led halyards do look nice at the dock during a boat show.

The cockpit is already a cluttered place without adding two halyards and a couple of reefing lines. I have sailed many boats whose cockpits are a bowl of linguini, with color-coded strings everywhere. Usually, the lines get dropped down the companionway into the cabin to get them out of the way. Soon they ensnare the cook and the navigator as well as the skipper.

If a boat has a low-friction arrangement that actually works and good storage pockets for the line tails, cockpit-led halyards and reefing lines are convenient, but try it before you buy it. I think it's simpler to just walk to the mast when it's necessary to raise, lower or reef the mainsail. A roller-furling jib is usually set at the beginning of the season and left in place, so its halyard should always be cleated at the mast.

A light-air headsail can change a boring day into a pleasant one. Before we equipped our boat with a poleless cruising spinnaker, we ran the engine on those long, hot downwind runs when the wind was less than ten knots. It's not fun to creep along at one or two knots with the mainsail and jib, especially in midsummer.

The cruising chute changed that. Now, CRESCENDO slips along comfortably in light air, reaching or running quietly while the autopilot steers and we lounge in the cockpit, looking about for traffic every five minutes, and enjoy music or books. It's a splendid ride, with only the rustling sound of water instead of the rumble of an engine.

The name given to these poleless spinnakers varies from one sailmaker to another, but the principle is the same for all. They are made of lightweight nylon; I can carry the bag with our 850-square-foot. chute with one hand. A "sock" encloses the sail until it is time to unfurl. Setting the chute entails raising it in its sausage-like sock, attaching the sheets and tack downhaul, and pulling a line to slide the sock up to the top and out of the way. Dousing it is equally simple; pull the furling line and the chute is encased in its envelope. When whitecaps appear on the water (about 12 knots of wind), I drop the cruising chute. I could drive the boat harder and get lots of speed, but this is cruising and cruising shouldn't require work.

Get a boat designed by a good naval architect and it will have a suitable rig. While it's fun to debate sloop vs. cutter or ketch vs. yawl with friends at the local marina, the decision isn't any more important than choosing four cylinders or six for your car, where either type will work just fine.

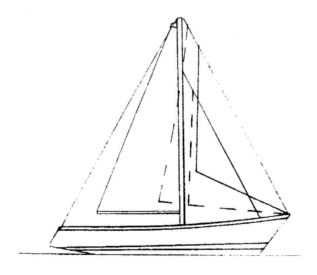

Cutter

The Cruising Sailor by Tom Dove

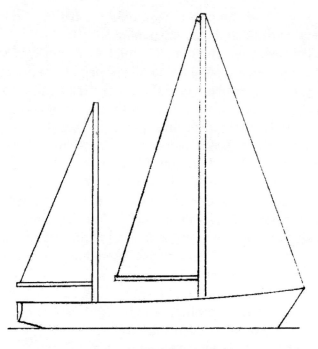

Ketch

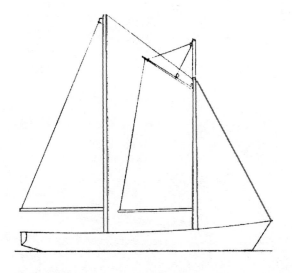

Schooner

The Cruising Sailor by Tom Dove

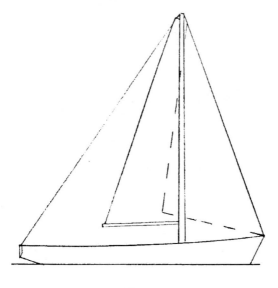

Sloop

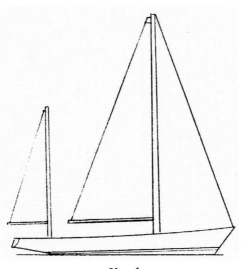

Yawl
Arthur Edmunds
Figure 7

The above illustrations represent different rigs.

The Cruising Sailor by Tom Dove

Chapter 4
The Mid-Size Cruiser

The three of them held their private thoughts as they watched the western sky transmute itself through shades of red and purple toward darkness. Sunset held a different meaning in the cockpit of a sailboat in the Atlantic Ocean than from a back porch, safely ashore. At sea, sunset was, inexorable.

There was no turning back from this small adventure, an overnight passage from Atlantic City, along the New Jersey coast and into New York harbor. It meant being alone on the ocean, with nothing to the east but Portugal and only one usable harbor to the west among those miles of sandy beach. This was the old coastal trade route, plied by thousands of ships, barks, brigs, brigantines and schooners since the seventeenth century; hundreds had been lost. Lights from the tall buildings ashore, five miles away, somehow added to the sense of isolation.

Tonight's forecast was favorable: the sky was clear, the wind a steady 12-knot southerly and the boat well prepared. They had dropped the big genoa and set the working jib so there should be no need to go onto the foredeck in the dark for a sail change. They rigged jacklines the length of the boat to provide a secure place to clip their safety harness lifelines and double-checked all the rigging for chafe. The batteries were fully charged, the tricolor navigation light at the masthead was lit and WINDY, a 1976 Ranger 33 sloop, reached easily across the long ocean swells, making just over five knots toward the northeast.

The Cruising Sailor by Tom Dove

The family had sailed WINDY together on the Chesapeake for years, slipping into quiet anchorages, riding out thunderstorms, racing with the local sailing club, exploring waterfront towns and collecting an abundance of memories. Three of them were aboard now; 14-year-old Kevin was eager to make this trip. His older sister, Jill had understandably become more interested in things her friends were doing ashore that summer and had opted to stay behind with relatives. Both she and her brother had been shaped by the responsibilities that came with cruising and she would later remember the experiences fondly. They missed her, both for companionship and seamanship, for she had become an agile, skilled sailor during their years of cruising the coast. She could be counted upon to hold a steady course, spot traffic and keep the boat moving well when she held the wheel.

Jim thought back to their worst-ever day of cruising. They had spent the summer cruising Long Island Sound and were returning to the Chesapeake via Delaware Bay, a notoriously fickle body of water. A cold front had passed through the night before and a booming northwesterly wind now roared down the bay at 25-30 knots. The tide was flooding, so he figured the favorable current would offset the beat to windward from Cape May to the C&D canal, fifty miles away. As usual, he had an alternative destination, the Cohansey river, about halfway up the bay on the New Jersey side. The first few years of cruising had taught him the value of the adage, "Always have a way out."

It didn't look too bad at first. They rigged for rough weather before leaving the harbor and entered Delaware Bay with a deep-reefed mainsail, a reefed working jib, foul-weather gear, safety harnesses and PFDs for all hands. Everything in the cabin was carefully stowed against being thrown about.

But they were not ready for the vicious seas created by wind against current. Six-foot waves marched relentlessly toward the sea, each rank less than two boat lengths behind the other. This close spacing meant that WINDY's bow was pointing downward from one wave as the next came on it. They took solid water over the bow and across the decks. The canvas dodger sheltered the cockpit from the worst of it, but sheets of spray soon covered them all.

They were not in serious danger -- a good boat will always stand more than its crew -- but it was tiring work. Even with reduced sail, WINDY heeled 30 degrees in the wind and nobody could concentrate longer than about an hour on the steering before requiring relief. Bulkheads creaked against the hull and water seeped around ports and toerail bolts. After six hours of this punishment, the tide turned against them and began pushing them back to Cape May. It was time to head for the alternate port and they slipped into the shelter of the Cohansey river with gratitude.

Everything below was wet; he vowed to caulk the offending cabin leaks as soon as they got home. His wife, Anne, declared it was time for a "lay day" in a marina to dry out, walk on solid ground and enjoy a hot meal in a restaurant.

He thought about the difference between the two children that day. Jill was plucky and determined, steering the boat accurately between the biggest waves and doggedly standing her entire watch without help. Kevin -- perhaps because he was younger and perhaps because he was feeling seasick for the first time -- spent much of his time lying down and trying to get comfortable.

The memory troubled Jim. How would this young teenage boy react to this first overnight passage along the coast? Could he handle the boat alone, or would he and Anne exhaust themselves supervising him all night?

They never stood specific watches during daylight, but traded the helm at intervals decreed by Anne, whom they all called the Official Comfort Committee. When the children were young, it was she who made certain that neither monopolized the most comfortable seat, or neglected galley and cleanup duties. As a result, they were a family team and that attitude carried over to the household. Years later, Jill would say of certain unruly peers, "You know, they need rules, just like we had when we were kids."

Now it was time to set the night watches. Jim and Anne had made a passage on a friend's boat from Bermuda to Annapolis and found the four-hour on, four-hour off schedule tiring, so they set two-hour watches for this night, with Jim on call at any time. Anne took the early watch from 10 PM to midnight, he sailed from midnight to 2 AM. Kevin wanted the 0200-0400 watch because he rarely got the opportunity to be awake at those hours. Dad would take over at 0400, when they should be approaching Sandy Hook and New York.

The boat was set up well for night sailing and for offshore passages with a small crew. They had often gone out at night in familiar waters at home, identifying the lights that winked on ashore and on buoys at sunset, and observing the gradual change from familiar daytime to the strangeness of the dark. The navigation station held the chart book on a plotting board; both could be moved to the cockpit when only one person was on watch. A protractor arm on the board allowed the skipper to plot positions and courses easily and a red chart light preserved night vision. The compass light was also red, the helmsman carried a small red flashlight, and a strict rule forbade turning on any white lights while sailing in the dark. They all knew even a short flash of white light would desensitize their vision and it took at least ten minutes for their eyes to again adapt to darkness.

There were three good sea berths in the cabin. The forward Vee berths were unusable at sea because the boat's motion was severe in that area. A settee to starboard had a lee cloth to keep the sleeper in place. The dinette also had a lee cloth. The quarter berth, which stretched out underneath the starboard cockpit seat, was snug and especially handy to the nav table and the cockpit. Jim took the quarter berth, where he could consult with the one on watch without disturbing the third crew member, who slept on the settee for this passage.

The Cruising Sailor by Tom Dove

Jim always found it difficult to sleep at sea; perhaps it was the feeling of responsibility that devolved upon him as skipper of the vessel. He woke several times during Anne's watch to take a look around and by the end of his own time at the wheel was quite tired. Handing over control to Kevin, at 0200, he explained the compass course, the landmarks that would appear ashore and told him to check the chart on the nav table at half-hour intervals. He rechecked the autopilot and went below.

He woke suddenly, not because anything startled him, but because an internal alarm clock triggered his brain. Glancing at the cabin clock, he quickly clambered out of the bunk and stumbled up through the companionway.

"Hi, Dad," Kevin said brightly. "Sleep well?"

"You didn't call me for my 4 AM watch," Jim replied. "I slept right through it."

"You looked like you needed some rest. Everything's under control. There's Ambrose Light three miles ahead and we have ships at eleven o'clock and two o'clock, inbound to New York. They'll pass ahead of us."

He looked around to confirm the news, smiling at the brightening eastern sky and at the realization that his son had suddenly grown up. When did that happen? Overnight? Maybe.

"Let me get some coffee and I'll take it. Thanks, kid," he said.

"No problem. It's been fun."

Coffee cup in hand, Jim looked at the chart table and noted Kevin had plotted GPS fixes each half hour, maintaining the proper distance offshore. Then, he noticed something else.

"You took three bearings and drew Lines Of Position for a fix?"

"Yeah. It's not very good, though. Those buildings and towers look an awful lot alike and it's hard to hold the binocular compass steady on the right one," Kevin replied.

"It's not bad at all. You can't expect it to match the

GPS exactly. How did you learn to do that?"

"Watched you. Read a few books."

The sails were drawing well and Kevin had turned off the autopilot and steered by hand for the last hour, just to enjoy the sensation of sailing.

"You know, Dad, we could go east of Long Island and make Block Island in another day instead of going through the Sound."

Jim looked at his son, trying to decide whether he was serious or just teasing. Kevin grinned and said, "But it would be nice to get a real night's sleep."

So they turned WINDY parallel to the shipping lanes and motorsailed past the Statue of Liberty and the Battery. When the four of them made this trip two years earlier, they had taken a mooring in Sheepshead Bay but this time the currents looked too favorable to miss, so they dropped the sails and motored under the Brooklyn Bridge, through Hell Gate and into Long Island Sound.

At a yacht club mooring in Manhasset Bay, tiredness came over them all by sundowner time and they mutually agreed that simple hors d'oeuvres would be just the thing for supper. The club's cannon boomed and they struck the colors. Yachting tradition was a nice thing.

Tomorrow would bring new harbors to explore, new currents to decipher and the beginning of another adventure in new waters, with the knowledge that there were now three competent sailors aboard.

The Boat

Like many men, Jim wanted the ability to sail offshore. When he and Anne bought this boat, he had held the idea that someday they would make extended ocean voyages, but discovered over the years that he preferred coastal cruising. The ocean passages on friends' vessels had been interesting and the steady winds and long waves invigorating, but the challenge of coastal navigation with its variable currents and weather and the peace of remote anchorages held even more appeal. He was glad now that they had not bought a heavy displacement voyager with limited sail area. Like most production cruiser/racers of her cra, WINDY was of moderate displacement, with a D/L of 259 and had an SA/D ratio of 17.7 for adequate power. They often used the big asymmetrical spinnaker on the Chesapeake to glide along in the typical 8-12 knot zephyrs of summer and the 135% genoa was normally at home on the forestay. A typical family boat, he concluded, was the best all-around choice for most sailors.

This boat was also comfortable and safe. Her motion always seemed easy, except for those notable days of bashing into steep, six-foot seas on Delaware Bay and similar times at the mouth of the Potomac, when any vessel her size would have taken a beating. It was no surprise when he calculated that the Comfort Value was a relatively high 28 and the Capsize Screening Value was a reassuring 1.75. Her speed was good; they conservatively planned for a five-knot average over a day's run and consistently made closer to six.

Other boats met the design and construction criteria and had made the final list of shopping choices, so the decision came down to interior layout and price. There was a lovely Morgan 34, whose centerboard would have been very welcome in many shallow anchorages; a Cal 34, which had a family resemblance to the Ranger and a beautiful Tartan 30; a Sabre 34 was appealing, but more expensive. All were used boats; Jim and Anne had decided against the much higher cost of a new vessel, balancing that against the slightly higher maintenance needs of an older model.

Anne understood the need for comfort and safety when cruising. She liked their boat's sizable, enclosed head compartment (although it seemed small now in comparison to new boats), plentiful enclosed storage space and good grab rails and secure footing all around the cabin. She also was happy with the relatively narrow cockpit. Many new boats, she found, were so wide that she could not brace herself adequately in rough conditions. Safety also meant visibility and good footing on deck. Anne's 5'3" height was a handicap in boats with high cabin tops, and low-cut racing genoas blocked critical vision forward for everybody in the crew. They had looked at some salty motorsailers like the Fisher 34 with deep cockpits that were hard to climb out of onto the decks and which had high bows that blocked the view forward. All those traits were unacceptable, although they were probably welcome to tall folks who sailed the North Sea.

WINDY's hull was deep enough for good stowage space beneath the settees and it had a bilge sump that collected the inevitable water that came aboard; many newer boats had wide, shallow hulls that lacked stowage for food and supplies. The shelves in WINDY's cabin were spacious but open; a boat carpenter enclosed them with sliding plastic doors to keep items from spilling when the boat heeled. The nav station was excellent for a boat this size, with chart stowage in the table, a convenient seat formed by the end of the quarter berth and space for mounting electronics.

WINDY had flaws. The side decks were narrow, a tradeoff for maximum cabin space below, but at least there was a fairly high toerail to keep a foot from slipping over. They added grab rails to the sides of the dodger for security when moving forward. The cockpit locker was spacious but unorganized and objects could fall against the engine or drive shaft. They partitioned off the engine compartment and added hangers for dock lines, fenders and a boat hook. The lazarette was accessible only through the cockpit locker and there appeared to be no cure for that, so some storage space would always be wasted.

Jim understood engines and electronics, but was not a skilled carpenter. He had read the magazine articles and books by those who could do fine joinery and admired their results, but had little luck with it himself. He finally reasoned that it made more sense to work at his regular job and make enough money to pay a craftsman to do some of the boat work properly. Top priorities were the icebox, the wiring and some interior carpentry. Several boatyards on the Chesapeake specialized in renovating old boats. He had found an excellent one to do the upgrades that would transform their standard boat into a semi-custom, small yacht.

As on most production boats, the icebox lacked good insulation and was too large. The result of this unfortunate combination was that ice melted rapidly, making frequent stops at marinas necessary. Jim and Anne had decided against refrigeration because it consumed too much electrical power and would require them to run the engine too often. They had a good boat carpenter rip out the icebox, re-insulate it with sheets of polyisocyanruate foam covered with foil to reflect heat, then seal the remaining voids with spray foam from cans. This was a big project, but now if they also used an insulating blanket inside the box, two or three blocks of ice would last for a week in midsummer.

At the same time, the carpenter removed the old pressurized alcohol two-burner stove top and installed a gimbaled Origo non-pressurized stove with an oven. Propane would have been a hotter, cheaper fuel, but both of them were wary of it and they did not cook extensively when cruising. Each summer brought one or two reports of boats lost to propane explosions on the Bay, and that's the reason it is prohibited on Coast Guard inspected passenger vessels.

The original electrical panel was inadequate, with only a few circuits for lights. Modern electronics, good cabin fans, more lights and a solar panel to keep the house batteries topped up were needed. The wires themselves were not tinned and they had corroded. It was time for a new panel and ABYC-grade wiring, so he had everything ripped out and replaced. It was expensive, but a good investment in safety and convenience. Now, they had spare circuits for any accessory they could imagine and the tinned, corrosion-resistant wires ran in neat bundles and looms to proper connectors. A battery monitor tracked electrical usage, an oversize alternator pumped electrons back into the heavy-duty golf cart batteries rapidly and AC circuits fed appliances when dockside.

The engine compartment was the WINDY's great weakness and there was no acceptable solution to the problems it caused. They enlarged an access opening near the carburetor, insulated the box with lead-lined foam and installed a light, but working on the engine would always be an exercise in contortion. Jim had tinkered with the engine long enough that he could always repair it, even in the tight quarters, but he mumbled harsh words for the boat's designer when it was time to change a water pump impeller.

The power plant was an Atomic Four, the venerable gas engine still found in tens of thousands of sailboats. Gasoline is more combustible than diesel fuel and therefore more dangerous on a boat, but actual incidents of explosions or fires from the A-4 are extremely rare; most gasoline accidents are on motorboats. It is a smooth, quiet, odorless engine and it ran reliably with minimal maintenance. Repowering with a diesel would cost over $9000, while rebuilding the A-4 cost around $2000. Perhaps someday they would repower, but it was not a top priority. Anyway, this engine was dead simple and Jim could repair and tune it easily. It reminded him of his first car, which lacked the electronics and vacuum hoses of newer models and had taught him the basics of engine maintenance.

So this was their little ship. She wasn't perfect, but she was very good for their purposes and they had worked out ways around the shortcomings in the years they had owned her. Although they had developed a strong emotional attachment to WINDY, any of a dozen other designs would have served them as well.

The Cruising Sailor by Tom Dove

Chapter 5
Talking About Boats

By the Numbers

No matter what glossy advertisements or proud owners say, the real nature of a boat is shown by a few calculated values used by all naval architects. Weight, power, speed, stability and comfort can all be expressed as numbers. Without lapsing to any elaborate mathematics, you can look at these numbers and get a good idea if a particular boat is meant to coastal cruise, cross oceans or daysail. You can even judge whether it will suit your own performance preferences.

The numbers won't say much about beauty; we all know where that is perceived.

Weight

A boat's weight is given as its Displacement, the weight of the water it displaces when floating at its normal waterline. In practice, the builder gets that number by weighing the boat on large scales. The stated displacement is usually without any gear, crew or stores aboard, although some companies will give a half-load displacement, which is a better indicator of the boat's actual weight in sailing trim.

Displacement tells us little except what size trailer or Travelift we need to carry the boat. It doesn't indicate whether the vessel is average, light or heavy, compared to other boats the same size. For that, we need a number called the Displacement-to-Length Ratio (D/L). The formula for calculating D/L is in Appendix 1.

The D/L is one of the best indicators of the builder's intent. It tells whether the designer was engineering a sports car or a truck.

A boat with a D/L of 300 or more is heavy for its length. One with a D/L below about 150 is light. Anything in the middle is moderate. Note that we mean LWL, not LOA, when talking about length in this context.

TABLE OF DENSITIES	
Aluminum	165 lbs/ft^3
Bronze	480 to 520 lbs/ft^3
Canned Food	50 lbs/ft^3
Sodas in 12oz	42 lbs/ft^3
Ferro-Cement	165 lbs/ft^3
Copper	550 lbs/ft^3
Glass Fiber	96 lbs/ft^3
Gasoline	46 lbs/ft^3
Diesel Fuel	53 lbs/ft^3
Lead	700 lbs/ft^3
Oak	52 lbs/ft^3
Fir Plywood	36 lbs/ft^3
Steel	490 lbs/ft^3
Window glass	160 lbs/ft^3
Fresh water	62.4 lbs/ft^3
Sea Water	64 lbs/ft^3

Arthur Edmunds
Figure 8

A designer will use the above item density information to arrive at the approximate boat weight for the completed boat. As an owner makes changes and adds stores to the boat, these weights should be kept in mind to maintain proper boat trim.

The Cruising Sailor by Tom Dove

Over time, boats have gotten progressively lighter. In the 1970s, a boat with D/L of 200 was light, but many production vessels today are in the 150-200 range. Ultralight racers often have D/L ratios well below 100; better materials have made this possible. Sandwiched composites and new reinforcing materials can be extremely strong, yet very lightweight. An old axiom held that boats were priced by the pound, like steak. That's no longer true.

So what? The water floats the boat, regardless of its weight, so what's the difference?

Heavy boats can carry loads easily without much change in their performance. Adding 1000 pounds to a 20,000 pound boat is much less significant than putting the same weight into a 5,000 pound vessel. This is the reason light-displacement craft like multihulls are so fast when empty and so slow when heavily laden.

Heavy boats require more power, either from sails or engine to accelerate, so a heavy boat will be slow in light air unless it carries a lot of sail. That means more work for the crew. In the blustery trade winds where plenty of power is available, the sails can be small and easily manageable, but such a vessel will be under-rigged for coastwise sailing.

In coastal conditions, a light boat is usually significantly faster than a heavy boat, unless it is overloaded. It will accelerate more easily and stay near its maximum speed more of the time in the light to moderate winds. On a long offshore passage, the heavy vessel may do as well as an overloaded light one. Racing boats are always as light as possible.

Heavy boats have a slower motion in waves. When a wave hits a heavy boat, the vessel does not respond immediately. Many people find this sort of motion less nauseating than the quicker motion of a light craft. Plowing through waves instead of bouncing over them means more spray is likely to come aboard the heavy craft than a light one, although, hull shape plays a large role in a boat's wetness on deck.

Light boats are more responsive to rudder and sail adjustments than heavy boats. This makes them more fun to sail in light to moderate wind conditions, but usually more work to steer when on a passage of several days. Long-range voyagers have traditionally preferred heavy boats as much for their self-steering ability as for their easy motion in a seaway or ability to carry lots of stores, but modern autopilots have removed much of that advantage.

Because the trend is toward lighter vessels, heavy boats generally look more traditional, while light ones look more modern. As with people, big boats can carry heavy D/L ratios better than small ones. A 40-footer with a D/L of 350 does not necessarily appear bulky, while the same D/L on a 25-footer can make it look hefty.

Power

Power comes from sail area. Sails are solar machines that convert the sun's energy (in the form of wind) to propulsion. The bigger the machine, the more power.

Since a heavy vessel requires more power to drive it than a light one, it would be nice to have a number that relates sail power to weight, giving us an idea of the actual performance of the boat. We have one. It's called the Sail Area/Displacement Ratio (SA/D). The formula is in Appendix 1.

It can be tricky to measure the sail area. The standard method reports the mainsail area plus 100 percent of the foretriangle, as if the jib exactly filled that space. We use the 100 percent measurement of the foretriangle because that's the only way to compare boats fairly; any boat can be fitted with a variety of jibs.

Sailors generally use genoa jibs that overlap the mainsail and have a length perpendicular to the luff that is about 125 to 150 percent of the foretriangle measurement. That's what is meant by a "125" or "150" jib. To complicate the matter, the foot of one 150-percent genoa jib may sweep low along the deck, while another sail with the same overlap may be cut much higher for better visibility but with a loss of sail area.

SA/D ratios typically fall in the 16-18 range. A value of 20 or higher indicates a very powerful sail plan, while anything below about 15 is quite tame. A few motorsailers have ratios near 10; you can assume that the motor will be running most of the time.

Since ocean winds are generally stronger than coastal breezes, a boat that is rigged for a comfortable average speed offshore often does not have enough sail area to move well on bays and sounds near shore. Likewise, boats from rugged sailing places like the North Sea usually are under-rigged for North American waters. Some American builders make two models: one for windy San Francisco Bay and one for the rest of the country.

For the whole picture, look at the D/L ratio as you consider SA/D numbers. A boat with a D/L of 100 (lightweight) and a SA/D of 21 (high power) will be a screamer. One with a D/L of 400 (heavy) and a SA/D of 14 (low power) will need a gale to move.

Speed

Every boat appears to have a speed limit it cannot exceed, no matter how much power you apply. The limit depends on the type of boat. Cruising sailboats generally have displacement hulls that plow through the water instead of planing hulls that skim across the surface. It is easy to calculate the limiting speed of such a hull.

The top speed of a displacement hull is limited by the wave it creates as it moves through the water; the boat cannot escape from the wave it makes. Long waves travel faster than short waves, so long boats, which can make long waves, travel faster than short boats. The simple formula is in Appendix 1.

For example, a Penguin class sailing dinghy or a 12-

The Cruising Sailor by Tom Dove

foot rowboat is limited to a hull speed of about 4.64 knots without planing. My Ranger 33 cruising sailboat has a waterline length (LWL) of about 27 feet and a corresponding hull speed of about 6.96 knots. A 40-foot boat with an LWL of 34 feet would top out around 7.81 knots.

There is one complication. A typical sailboat changes its waterline length as it heels over in a breeze and its overhangs fore and aft become submerged. As the LWL becomes longer, the boat can go faster. Thus, the reported LWL may not be the true waterline length when the boat is underway. Some clever designers use the stern overhang for additional length even when the boat is upright; our CRESCENDO adds nearly three feet in waterline length as its stern wave builds higher. That increases its potential speed by half a knot.

Friction is also a factor. At low speeds, the drag of water molecules across the underwater surface is greater than wave making resistance, so designers take care to keep wetted surface to a minimum to insure good light air performance. Surface friction is higher on a rough surface than a smooth one. You will see a big drop in light-air performance if barnacles grow on the hull during the warm season.

If enough power is available to drive a displacement hull to its limiting speed, it will run at that speed and no faster. Adding more power simply makes a bigger wake. A 400 horsepower engine in our 33-footer would generate some huge bow and quarter waves, perhaps enough to swamp the boat, but it would not go faster. Historical accounts tell of heavy ships being driven under their own bow waves and sinking because they carried too much sail power.

If the hull design permits it to rise onto its bow wave and skim across the water like a skipping oyster shell, displacement hull speed is no longer the limit. A planing boat will go faster with increased power until friction or instability finally become the barriers.

Planing hulls are common in runabouts, lightweight outboard skiffs and high performance sailing dinghies, but

The Cruising Sailor by Tom Dove

even many displacement boats can plane for short distances if conditions are perfect. We have enjoyed some exciting surfing down large waves on our boat, occasionally touching 12 knots. A following sea and 25-knot wind on Albemarle Sound gave us a seven-hour run at over eight knots average, an exciting day spent well above our theoretical hull speed.

Multihull boats, like catamarans and trimarans, are fast for a different reason. Their hulls are long and very narrow, so they do not create waves large enough to limit the speed of the boat. Once the ratio of length to beam exceeds about 10:1, the hull speed formula no longer applies. Monohull boats typically have a length to beam ratio between 3:1 and 4:1.

For a cat or a tri to go fast, it must be light. Once those hulls are buried deep in the water, they do create speed-limiting waves and also gain wetted surface. Multihull cruisers must exercise strict self control over the quantity of stores they bring aboard.

That's a major reason for the discrepancy between the performance of racing multihulls and cruising models. Owners of a cruising cats and tris report actual speeds about 25 percent above comparable monohulls, not the radical double-digit velocities of the world record setters. This is still a useful increase in speed and multihulls have other advantages like more interior space and a flat ride.

Average speed is generally more important than top speed. It takes a lot more power to get that last fraction of a knot from a displacement-hull boat, so we normally cruise about six knots in our 33-footer, either at half throttle on the engine or under full sail in a typical 12-knot breeze. To reach the limiting speed, I must run the engine at a much higher speed or drive the boat hard under full sail in a strong wind, which is fun occasionally but tiring as a general practice. It's more comfortable to take it easy and comfort is an essential part of cruising.

That's a fundamental difference between cruising and racing. While the racer carries sails that will drive the boat at full speed in the lulls and tolerates overpowering in the puffs, the cruiser rigs for the puffs and accepts lower speed in the lulls for the sake of comfort.

Stability

For most landlubbers, the less "tipping" the boat does, the better and for any sailor, right side up is much better than upside down. But a sailboat that doesn't heel over when the wind fills its sails really doesn't feel much like a sailboat and heeling also works as a safety valve to dissipate the excess force from strong puffs of wind. We need a compromise between the pleasant sensation of sailing and stability. We also need to know the boat will return to its upright position once a strong gust has ended or a big wave has passed.

A boat that does not heel when side forces act on it is said to be "stiff." One that heels easily is called "tender." These traits are only partially related to a boat's ability to right itself when completely turned over by wind or waves, which is called its "ultimate stability." Stiffness results from wide beam (including the widely spaced double or triple hulls of a catamaran or trimaran), deeply placed ballast (lead at the end of a deep keel) and a hull with sharp-edged bilges, like a barge. Tender boats often have narrow beam, shoal draft and a slack (gently rounded) hull shape.

You may think everybody would want a stiff boat, but that neglects the comfort factor and sometimes, ultimate stability. Military ships, racing boats with deep ballasted keels and catamarans are stiff, so they bounce back quickly from any heeling motion. This quick motion can be stressful. The seasoned sailors who ran the ferry across the Bay of Fundy from Maine to Nova Scotia were seasick for a week after their familiar, rolling ship was replaced by a stiff, 300-foot, high-speed catamaran.

Passenger liners and round-bottomed cruising boats can be pushed over by waves or wind, then they recover

The Cruising Sailor by Tom Dove

slowly to an upright position. Many people find that kind of slow rolling motion less nauseating than a quick roll, but some do not.

Cruising sailboats often are initially tender, then they stiffen as the heeling angle increases. Many sailors find this trait a good compromise that combines the pleasant sensations of sailing with an easy motion and limited heeling.

Heeling may surprise you the first time you sail, but you are less likely to be afflicted by seasickness on a sailboat than on a motorboat. While a motorboat rolls constantly from side to side, a sailboat is stabilized by the wind and holds its angle of heel more steadily.

The only way to determine your own motion preferences is by trying a variety of boats yourself, although conversations with other sailors can be illuminating. A method for calculating roll time is in Appendix 1.

You and your mate may disagree; I like to sail catamarans, but my wife, Pam, does not. She loves to feel a boat heeled down to its best lines in a fresh breeze and rushing through the waves and cats don't do that. They simply stand upright and go.

While stiffness or tenderness under sail is largely a question of preferences, ultimate stability is a safety item. If the worst happens and the boat capsizes, it should right itself.

The best measure of ultimate stability is the Range of Positive Stability, which tells how far you can knock the boat down and still expect it to roll back upright. An ocean cruiser should have a Range of Positive Stability of at least 120 degrees from vertical, while a coastal cruiser can have somewhat less. Calculating this value is not simple and many builders do not publish it. You can find the numbers for your own boat from US Sailing (see Appendix 2 for address), if your design is raced under the International Measurement System (IMS) rule. The Range of Positive Stability is used in the IMS racing rating formula, but there is a fee for this service.

The Screening Value is a short way to get a ballpark

idea of a boat's stability range. US Sailing devised this calculation after the Fastnet Race disaster to eliminate extreme designs from ocean racing. The formula is in Appendix 1. A value below 2 is desirable for offshore sailing safety. Remember that it is an approximation based on limited data, not a precise tool, so you cannot presume that a vessel rating 1.9 is five percent better than one that rates 2.0. Plenty of good coastal cruisers rate higher than 2 by the Screening Formula; they simply may be marginal or undesirable designs for stormy oceans.

Comfort

I mentioned roll time as an indicator of comfort at sea. Designer Ted Brewer has spent a lot of time thinking about seakindliness. His Comfort Value incorporates length, bow and stern overhangs and beam to predict how quickly a boat will return to a vertical position, either when being rolled from side to side or when plowing into a sea. The formula is in Appendix 1. It's not perfect, but it will give you an idea of the suitability of a particular boat for cruising in rough waters. Bigger boats generally rate higher in comfort.

A lightweight, beamy, modern 28-footer like a Beneteau, Catalina or Hunter will have a Comfort Value around 17, while a sizable vessel with a long waterline and traditional hull shape like the Crealock 40 rates about 37 and the big Taswell 72 is nearly 50. A high number indicates a gentle, slow motion in waves, both from side to side and fore and aft, while a low number means a bouncier ride. Most popular production cruising boats in the 30-40 foot range have values in the mid and upper 20s. I consider our 33-foot CRESCENDO seakindly for her size and her rating is 28.

The Cruising Sailor by Tom Dove

Putting it Together

The easiest way to assemble all the information for a variety of boats is with a computer spreadsheet or a database that will do calculations. I list the categories across the top of a Claris Works spreadsheet, the boat names down the side and put the formulas into the columns of cells. I've also had good results with File Maker Pro, entering the data from published sources and making boxes with the formulas to give the calculated values.

There are sites on the Worldwide Web that will perform the calculations automatically and at least one of them maintains specifications and calculated values for a variety of vessels. As Web addresses are ephemeral, use one of the standard search engines, like Yahoo, Lycos, Excite or Google to find the URLs. Try "sailboat," "speed" and "calculations" as search criteria.

The Cruising Sailor by Tom Dove

Chapter 6
The Full-Size Cruiser

Thanks to the all-seeing eye of radar, the synthetic constellation of Global Positioning Satellites and plain old paper charts, combined with years of practice and a good dose of caution, TRAVELER a husky Dickerson 37 cruising boat rounded up in calendar-perfect Southwest Harbor, Maine. The morning fog was just burning off and the wind had not yet picked up to its normal afternoon force. Bill stood on the foredeck, anchor rode in hand, and his wife, Ruth, steered to the spot they had decided upon a few moments earlier.

His arm went horizontal, the signal for neutral on the engine, then up, the sign for reverse. She shifted the gears smoothly and the boat stopped, then began to move backwards; she compensated for the propeller's kick to port with a bit of right rudder. As the vessel backed slowly, he lowered the anchor and paid out chain and line until the precalculated amount was over the bow roller, then signaled for neutral again. As the anchor dug in, the line grew taut, the boat swung straight and they were secure. Another passage was complete.

After a month of cruising Nova Scotia, they had left Yarmouth in the morning, and had a fine sail in a southwest breeze across the mouth of the Bay of Fundy. They had switched over to their nighttime watch-keeping schedule of three hours on, three hours off, shortly before the fog rolled in. Throughout the night, targets on the radar blipped across to starboard and to port; vessels passing unseen but not unknown.

"At least the high-speed ferry out of Bar Harbor doesn't

run at night," Ruth noted as they changed watch at midnight. It had been a bit tense earlier that day when the 300-foot, black-hulled catamaran went roaring past at 41 knots. They had checked the ferry schedule and both captains were scrutinizing their radar screens as well as keeping a sharp lookout, but the two vessels passed less than a mile apart.

"Yep. That felt like flying a J-3 Cub through the airspace at New York," Bill said.

"Or commuting to work on the Beltway," she quipped.

They both smiled, having recently retired early from their jobs in their fifties in order to explore the coast by water while health was still on their side. Their children were out of college and their parents were still independent, so the window to adventure was open. This was their second year of extended cruising. While they had a compact condominium as a land base, they lived aboard most of the year, moving north and south with the seasons.

Now they were safe at anchor in a beautiful place and could wind down from alertness with a cup of hot chocolate before a long nap.

"Nothing like that anchorage on the Rhode River, is it?" he asked.

She grinned. That was their standing joke, their reference point for all that could go wrong with anchoring. It had been a remarkable, chaotic event and they remembered it clearly if not fondly.

That had been their first year with the new boat, although both had considerable experience in smaller craft. They carried over what they had learned from two-week cruises and club racing in light-displacement craft under 35 feet and found that everything transferred easily. A few charter trips on bigger boats had convinced them that they could manage TRAVELER.

It was a summer afternoon and VHF weather repeated its mantra for July, "Hot and humid today, with a chance of afternoon or evening thunderstorms, some with strong, gusty

The Cruising Sailor by Tom Dove

winds." As they reached across the Chesapeake and into the West River on a 15-knot southerly wind, ominous black clouds boiled over the western horizon.

It was time to find a protected place to anchor. They had planned to sail to Annapolis but their second choice, the Rhode River, was closer. They had learned how important it was to always have a way out -- a closer anchorage, a spare anchor, a smaller sail, an extra can of fuel.

They headed up, furled the mainsail and jib and motored into a good spot to ride out bad weather from the northwest, tucked under the lee of a cornfield near the river entrance. Only a few boats were there when they arrived, but the anchorage filled quickly with others as the afternoon wore on. When they set out crackers, cheese and drinks at "sundowner" time, the harbor was crowded and more boats were still arriving.

"Whoa! Look at this!" Bill wondered aloud, "Where's he going?"

A single-hander in an elderly Morgan 34 came into the creek under full sail, apparently unconcerned with the rest of the fleet. He raced straight into the middle of the anchored boats, locked the tiller straight, tossed an anchor and line off the stern and immediately braced himself against the companionway.

The anchor caught suddenly and the sloop stopped like a bungee jumper, springing back in a splash of water as the nylon rode rebounded. The single-hander was anchored.

"Looks like he's survived that maneuver a few times before," Ruth laughed. "I wonder how often he misses."

"What a zoo," he said. "Did you see the motorboat over there with just enough anchor line to touch the bottom?"

"Yes. Did you see the 45-footer with the 12-pound anchor? They must spend most of their time in marinas."

"How about the guy who pulled up ten feet from our starboard side and started to drop his hook? He seemed annoyed when I suggested he was too close. I guess he never heard of swinging when the wind shifts."

"I liked the three charter boats that came in together. The first one didn't shackle the anchor to the rode before tossing it overboard and the second didn't secure the rode to the cleat before dropping the anchor and all the line over. At least the third one got it right and they rafted alongside him."

"Maybe they'll all be OK, but I wouldn't count on it. Look at those clouds," he said.

"Better get some fenders ready," she added.

The storm struck as they usually do, with a 180 degree wind shift and a sudden blast of cold air from the north. In minutes, it was blowing 40 knots from the new direction.

As the fleet swung around to face the new wind, the high-sided boat with the undersized anchor began drifting away, its partying crew below deck unaware that they were underway. The motorboat with the short anchor rode also slipped off to leeward and would soon run aground on the opposite shore. The single-hander's boat held at first, then the anchor pulled loose, dragged 20 feet and reset just in time to miss another sailboat. A runabout ahead, which had dropped the hook too close just before the squall hit, swung dangerously close to TRAVELER. The couple held fenders near their bow to cushion any impact but worried more that the runabout would tangle in their anchor line. The motorboat skipper started his engine, picked up his anchor and moved closer to shore to reset it successfully.

Then came the rain, thousands of gallons of rain, dumped from the sky as if from a great waterfall. Visibility dropped to nothing. Bill and Ruth retreated to the shelter of the dodger and Bimini.

"There goes a dinghy," she said as an empty inflatable flipped over and over like a sheet of newspaper in the wind.

"There's another," he added as a pram drifted by. "I wonder if they'll all fetch up on the beach or if some will make it out into open water."

"Look! Somebody's coming in," she said, pointing

toward the Bay.

Sure enough, a 14-foot skiff with an outboard motor was slowly moving through the blowing rain toward their stern.

"Hey! Can I tie up behind you?" a voice called. "My anchor and rope blew away." Bill took the ragged line from the skiff's bow, cleated it to his stern and helped the two drenched occupants into their cockpit.

"Thanks. we were just out after rockfish and this storm came out of nowhere. You were lucky to be in here," one fisherman said. "Where is this, anyway?"

"Rhode River."

"Where's that?"

"Don't you have a chart?"

"Chart?"

"Like this," Ruth said, bringing up a chart book from the cabin. She opened it and pointed to the creek.

"That's a pretty map," the second fisherman said. "Where do you get one of those?"

Bill and Ruth looked at each other with an I-don't-believe-this look.

"Actually, I have an old one you can have, but get the latest edition when you get home," she said. "Try a marine supply store. Fishing supply places should have them, too."

One fisherman said, "We put in from a ramp on the Eastern Shore and were near a green buoy with a flashing white light on it. When the rain came, I started the motor and went toward the light. We ran for an hour and it disappeared near here. I wonder how that happened."

"Sounds like you followed the white stern light of a boat coming into this river. Lucky for you," Bill said.

"Thanks. I guess there's a lot to this boating stuff, huh?"

"Yeah. You might think about taking a course from the Coast Guard Auxiliary or Power Squadron this winter," Bill replied.

Chesapeake squalls are short-lived and an hour later it was calm and the western sky cleared just in time for a brilliant sunset. The fishermen motored away, rejuvenated with hot coffee and snacks and others of the fleet retrieved their lost dinghies, awnings, oars and cushions.

Later that evening, Bill and Ruth switched on the VHF radio and heard:

"Coast Guard, I'm headed North, my latitude is 38 degrees and my longitude is 76 degrees, 20 minutes. Where am I?" Long pause.

"Captain, you are in the Potomac river, going toward Washington."

"I can't be. I'm going to Ocean City."

It developed that the misplaced boat driver had left Norfolk, Virginia with a GPS receiver but without charts, taken a wrong turn in the rain at Hampton and headed up the Chesapeake Bay instead of out into the Atlantic ocean. When he reached the latitude he had written down for Ocean City, Maryland, he turned left and was surprised to find that the landscape was all wrong.

Bill and Ruth exchanged a look and laughed all the way through supper.

The Boat

TRAVELER is a 37-foot Dickerson, designed by George Hazen and built at the headwaters of La Trappe Creek on the Eastern Shore of Maryland. Bill and Ruth were the second owners; the first had gone transatlantic to the Mediterranean, cruised there for a year and returned via the tradewind route and the Caribbean islands. It was a proven, strong vessel, larger than its length overall would indicate and more like a 40-footer in handling, space and mass. While the profile above the water looks very traditional, with moderate overhangs and pleasant sheer, the underbody is modern, with a long fin keel. This reduces wetted surface and improves speed.

The Cruising Sailor by Tom Dove

Not a light-air flyer, it carried enough sail to make up for its weight with additional power and a cruising spinnaker pulled it along well in the gentle breezes of the Chesapeake summer. Some of these boats were ketch-rigged, but this sloop version had better speed and windward ability, although the couple occasionally wished for the handy mizzen mast as a place to mount the radar and Single Sideband radio antennas.

They had shopped seriously for a catamaran in the 40-foot range, but all the multihulls they found were expensive and most were battered from years of charter service in the Caribbean. Demand kept the prices high, much as they did for trawlers in the motorboat world and the couple found much better buys among the fleet of quality used monohulls.

Living aboard for several months at a time called for plenty of stowage space, strong construction, simple systems that would not require too much maintenance and room to carry on other hobbies. Ruth enjoyed crafts and knitting, Bill liked electronics and they both had sizable libraries of books.

The Dickerson 37 had an aft cockpit layout instead of a center cockpit with a private cabin aft. They liked center cockpit boats, but this hull was a bit narrow to carry off the design well because the aft cabin was too small for anything but a sleeping space. Their original search was for a center cockpit boat over 40 feet, but the Dickerson appeared on the market at the time and price they wanted, so they bought it.

Shallow draft was important for the Chesapeake and the Bahamas, as was reasonable air draft for the ICW. A reliable engine and plenty of water and fuel tankage were essential. This boat had them all, was small enough to be manageable by a middle-aged couple and stable enough to be a good working platform.

The Cruising Sailor by Tom Dove

The Cruising Sailor by Tom Dove

Chapter 7
Arriving & Staying Put

Anchors

Put any two cruising sailors together and the conversation will soon turn to anchors. No matter what their political orientations, all skippers are conservative about anchoring and slow to change their opinions.

I think of anchors in four categories: traditional hooks, plows, pivoting flukes and innovative. There are good anchors in each of these groups as well as poor ones. Traditional hooks like the fisherman or yachtsman anchors are not well suited to modern boats, except for rare, special bottom conditions, because they are heavy and hard to stow. They look great at the end of driveways and on wooden schooners, but most sailors today pick more efficient designs.

Plow anchors like the old standby CQR are strong and reliable in a wide variety of bottom conditions. Popularized by the Hiscocks in the 1950s, they remain the first choice of most serious world voyagers, especially the British. They are expensive. While they do not have immense holding power for their weight, they dig in quickly and reset reliably when a wind or current change swings the boat to a different direction.

Pivoting fluke anchors are spin-offs of the Danforth, widely used by the U.S. military after its invention about the time of World War II. With lots of holding area, they can develop substantial holding power for their weight and the flat design makes them easy to stow. They are probably the most common anchor found on American pleasure boats because they are inexpensive and adequate for day cruising or overnighting. They pull out when the direction of pull changes and they do not reset reliably. They will also foul easily on oyster shells or rocks and are not effective in weeds. I eventually got tired of waking up adrift after wind changes and switched to a different type of anchor.

Most modern anchors are derived from the plow, but have special contours to make them more efficient -- at least, it's supposed to work that way. I have had excellent results with the Delta, a non-pivoting update of the CQR and the Bruce and the Max, more distant cousins of the same hook. Practical Sailor newsletter reports encouraging results with the new Bulwagga and Spade anchors, but it will be years before they gain wide acceptance, even if they are very good.

My standard anchor on CRESCENDO is a 24-pound Max, which sets quickly, does not foul, resets on swinging and works on short scope when necessary. It's the best I've found. My secondary anchor, a 22-pound Delta, was formerly my primary hook. Now it's called to service as the second anchor in a Bahamian moor or whenever I must anchor by the stern. I do carry a big Pekny in the bilge, just in case. It is a take-apart version of the Northill anchor, a hooking-type device somewhat like the old Yachtsman that should be effective on rocky bottoms. The dinghy carries a five-pound Danforth, which is adequate for those minimal demands and is easy to carry with its rode in a small bag.

Several anchor types are illustrated at the end of this chapter.

The Chain-Rope-Chain-Rope rode

A sizable boat means a sizable anchor and that can mean heavy lifting. A typical 35 to 40-foot boat requires an anchor weighing at least 35 pounds and chain weighs about one pound per foot. If you follow the practice of world voyagers and use an all-chain anchor rode, the weight becomes oppressive. With an all-chain rode, you need a scope of 3:1; that is, the anchor rode is three times as long as the distance from the bottom of the harbor to the bow roller, so at least 80 pounds of steel is deployed in a 10-foot deep anchorage if your bow is five feet above the waterline.

You either get a windlass, which calls for heavy electrical wiring and another piece of machinery to maintain, or you find an alternative. I've found an alternative that works very well along the east coast of the U.S. Chafe might be a problem on rock or coral, but you shouldn't anchor in coral, anyway.

Courtesy of the Manufacturer
Figure 9

This model windlass has the motor mounted below the deck and the capstan with deck pipe above the deck. If you decide you need a windlass, this provides a clean uncluttered working area.

This is the Chain-Rope-Chain-Rope rode and it automatically lets you find the correct scope (about 5:1 for this rig), absorbs tugging shocks, adds weight to make the rode curve into a catenary to keep the pull on the anchor horizontal, and reduces hoisting effort. It also makes a two-anchor Bahamian moor a snap.

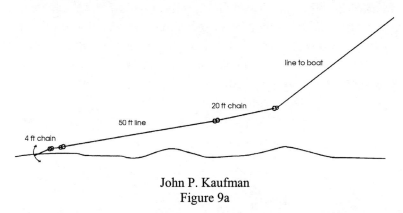

John P. Kaufman
Figure 9a

The Chain-Rope-Chain-Rope anchoring combination.

The anchor is attached to a short piece of chain (four or five feet), which is connected in turn to 50 feet of nylon line. The line goes to a half-boat length of chain, which attaches to the remainder of the nylon line (I carry about 150 feet). In our hypothetical 35 to 40-footer, the anchor is 35 pounds, the short chain 5 pounds and the long chain about 20 pounds. Nylon rope's weight is negligible.

To anchor in a typical ten-foot-deep harbor, let the first chain, the short nylon and the second chain out to the beginning of the long rode. That will be a five-to-one scope, including the height of the bow above the water of about five feet. For each foot of water depth over ten, let out one arm span of rode (five to six feet) to maintain the ratio. The long piece of chain provides a catenary weight and improves the angle of pull on the anchor.

In the morning, go forward slowly with the engine while hauling in the rode. The long, heavy chain is on deck by the time you are lifting the anchor, reducing the weight you must lift by nearly half. You will never need to lift more than about 40 pounds and most people can do that without a windlass.

For a Bahamian moor, which is useful in areas where the current reverses strongly, I shackle a second anchor, with its own 50 feet of nylon and short chain, to a swivel at the bottom of the main rode's long chain. I lower the main anchor part of the way, then walk to the stern and drop the second anchor. There is only one rode coming to the bow, so nothing gets twisted and the whole rig is easy to raise the next day.

This is not an original idea; I first saw it described by a cruiser in New Hampshire. It works with any kind of anchor.

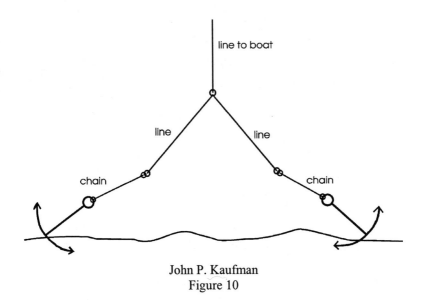

John P. Kaufman
Figure 10

The Bahamian moor. All connection points should use the correct combination of anchor shackles, thimbles and swivels. An additional length of chain and line rode can be added if you prefer the chain-rode-chain-rode combination, described in the text.

Docking

Early in your cruising life, you will need to pull up to a dock for fuel or into a marina slip for an overnight stay. To see the way NOT to do this, spend an hour watching folks coming and going at any fuel dock. Then, try the simple way.

Most boaters nose up to the dock, toss a bow line to the attendant who belays it to a piling, then spend the next several minutes figuring out how to get the boat parallel to the pier. It isn't easy to do, as the bow line severely restricts maneuverability of a single prop boat.

The same folks try to back into a slip by backing (or nosing) in without tying a line to anything first and usually take two or three tries, each time caroming off pilings, before they finally settle into place. It's embarrassing.

One piece of rope can cure these problems. It's called a spring line and it should be your first connection to shore.

When you pull up to a fuel dock, turn parallel to the pier, stop within arm's length and connect a rope from a piling to a cleat amidships on your boat, leaving several feet of slack. If your boat does not have midships cleats, use a jib sheet winch near the forward end of the cockpit. Now, your vessel is under control. Go forward slowly to take up the slack, turning the rudder away from the pier (port turn if starboard side to) and your boat will be drawn into the pier where you can attach the bow and stern lines at leisure. It's that simple; you can do it single-handed without an attendant on the dock. Before making the approach, hang a large fender over the side about where you expect the rub rail to contact the dock.

The Cruising Sailor by Tom Dove

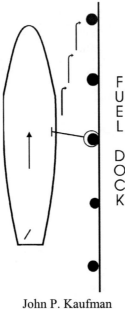

John P. Kaufman
Figure 11

Side to docking procedure.

    To enter a marina slip, pull up at right angles to the slip so your stern clears one outer piling by a couple of feet and the rub rail of your boat rests on a fender against the other piling. Loop a long rope around the piling where the fender is and bring both ends back to the cockpit, securing it to the jib sheet winch or a stern cleat. Now, back slowly against the tension of that spring line and watch your boat magically turn stern-first into the slip. It helps to have a crew member hold the fender in place. When the boat is aligned in the slip, loop lines from the bow to the two pilings forward and from the stern to two pilings or cleats on the pier and you're home for the night. Sometimes, you will need a second spring line to prevent the boat from drifting too far forward. Your stern is now close to the pier and you do not need to climb over the bow to go ashore, as those who entered bow-first must do.
    If you have a choice, take a slip or fuel dock approach

that permits you to fasten the spring line to the port side. Most boats kick to port under power and that will make your backing into the slip even smoother. Once in the slip, secure the windward (or up-current) bow and stern lines first.

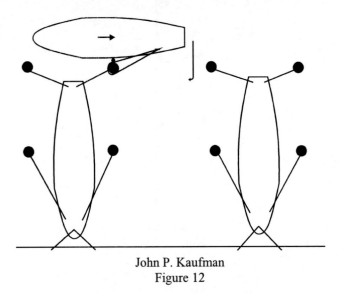

John P. Kaufman
Figure 12

Docking stern to in a slip.

    Next morning, cast off the leeward bow and stern lines first and pull forward to get underway. By looping the lines around the pilings, you do not have to untie anything and departure is smooth and easy. Effective use of a spring line calls for a sturdy rub rail, which should be standard equipment on any cruiser. If yours does not have a good rub rail, install one.
    I like large, flat rectangular fenders or fender boards because they cover a big surface and are easy to stow in a cockpit locker.
    There are infinite variations on these two basic docking techniques which you will learn with experience, but the simple spring line connection provides some time to think during the maneuvers and thus makes you look like a pro every time.

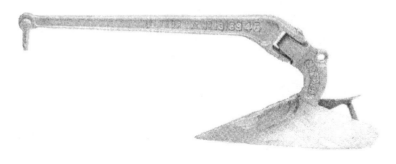

Courtesy of the Manufacturer
Figure 13

CQR anchor. Note the pivoting shank.

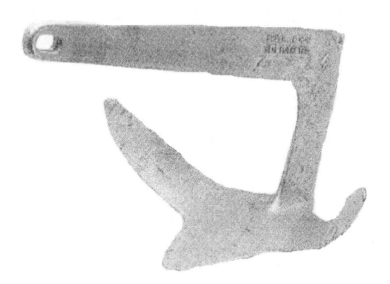

Courtesy of the Manufacturer
Figure 14

Bruce anchor.

The Cruising Sailor by Tom Dove

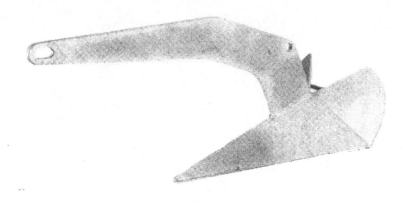

Courtesy of the Manufacturer
Figure 15

Delta anchor. This design does not use a pivot on the shank.

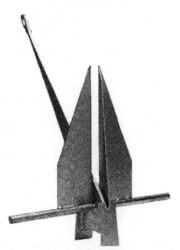

Courtesy of the Manufacturer
Figure 16

Danforth anchor.

Chapter 8
Soundness

When my two brothers and I were children, we enjoyed making papîer-mâché masks. One soaked strips of newspaper in flour-and-water paste and laid them across the other's face until it was completely covered with two or three layers. After a half hour to set, we removed the molded mask and painted it. It always fit perfectly, of course.

Building a fiberglass sailboat is just like that -- except the face becomes a plug for the hull or another part, the newspaper becomes fiberglass cloth and the flour-and-water paste becomes polyester or epoxy resin. There's also another step: using the "mask" or mold to build the boat parts.

Once the designer has finished, the builder makes a mockup, or plug, to the plans. He then fairs, smoothes and waxes the plug and laminates strips of fiberglass cloth and resin over it to make a female mold. When the mold is finished, factory workers build boats by laminating layers of fiberglass cloth and resin inside the mold, then popping the part free. Properly cared for, a mold can be used about 100 times. Thus, the initial expense is high, but the cost is amortized over the entire production run.

The deck and other parts are built in the same manner as the hull. It is not unusual for a mid-size cruising sailboat to have 30 or 40 separate molded fiberglass parts. These may include an interior cabin liner, hatches, a one-piece head compartment, cabinets and reinforcing beams. The quality of the boat begins with the quality of materials and care in the lay-up of the parts.

Arthur Edmunds
Figure 17

Male plug mold.

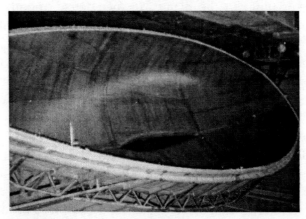

Arthur Edmunds
Figure 18

The Cruising Sailor by Tom Dove

Female mold.

The technology of materials constantly changes, usually for the better but with occasional setbacks like the blister disasters of the 1980s which resulted from formulation changes that caught boat builders unprepared. Some carefully constructed yachts of that era developed rashes of tiny blisters over their underwater areas when their builders switched to "improved" resins without testing them carefully first.

But change has generally been for the good of the breed. Many builders now use carbon fiber or aramid for reinforcement in critical areas, reducing weight and increasing strength. Vinylester resins under the surface gel coat layer make the hull less permeable to water and prevent blistering. Various weave patterns are used in specific areas to make them lighter or less flexible under load.

Many fiberglass laminates are cored to make them stronger and lighter, especially parts like decks and hatches. The core is simply a layer of closed-cell plastic foam, plastic beads, balsa or plywood laid into the mold atop the outer layers and sealed with an inner layer of glass and resin. Properly done, it makes a very rigid, lightweight part. Improperly done, it absorbs water, breaks apart and fails. The result depends entirely on the skill of the builder.

The best way to insure that the laminate layers are tightly bonded together, especially if they are cored, is to cover the part with a huge sheet of plastic and pump out the air inside. The procedure (vacuum bagging) forces the layers into close contact, without voids, or air spaces. An efficient variant of vacuum bagging is called the Seeman Composite Resin Infusion Molding Process (SCRIMP). The SCRIMP builder applies a gel coat to the mold, followed by a layer of chopped glass strands wetted in vinylester resin. Layers of glass cloth are applied dry to that surface, then the entire interior is covered with an airtight plastic membrane. Pumps remove the air from the layers of glass cloth and workers then inject a measured amount of resin at several points. Vacuum and capillary action draw the resin throughout the layers, so it saturates the glass to the optimum resin/glass ratio and eliminates all voids. The process also eliminates any release of styrene and other noxious vapors into the atmosphere, keeping the neighbors and the Environmental Protection Agency happy.

Molded fiberglass parts are very flexible but repeated flexing can make them crack and fail. The designer will create shapes that reinforce each other to make the entire boat rigid. This can be done in several ways and there is no one best method. Any properly designed, well-executed system can be effective, so it all goes back again to the skill of the designer and the care of the builder.

Older boats usually have an interior pan liner and structural plywood bulkheads for reinforcement. Some newer vessels have structural fiberglass grids, pioneered by Ericson Yachts as the "Triaxial Force Grid" to stiffen the hull. All boats rely on a secure bond between the hull and deck for rigidity, much as securing the top of a shoe box makes it a stiff structure instead of a flexible one.

Certain construction practices make it difficult to reach all interior areas of the hull. Many builders lay the wiring into the deck mold and then fasten the assembly to the hull mold, encasing the wiring so it is inaccessible for maintenance. A flooring or an overhead interior molding can prevent access to surfaces you need to repair. Look inside cabinets and other hidden areas of any boat you are considering and ask yourself, "How would I reach that fitting to re-bed it when it leaks?"

Fortunately, sailors are quality conscious and have complained to builders about the worst transgressions, such as covering undersides of decks with cheap carpeting and thus making bolts for deck fittings inaccessible. You still see such practices on most small powerboats. Poke around inside a production runabout or motor yacht, even some mid-priced popular ones, for a real eye-opening view into the world of cheapness.

The bonding between parts is critical. If a part, such as

a structural grid, is laid into the hull while the resins of the hull are still wet and the two parts cure together, it creates a primary bond. This is substantially stronger than the secondary bond that results from attaching a molded part to a hull which has already cured. It's impossible to assemble a boat fast enough to make all the bonds primary, but the crucial structural ones, such as internal grids, should be primary bonds.

Some builders create nonstructural parts, such as cabinetry, with chopped glass fibers and resin instead of hand laid cloth. This is cheaper and faster and is adequate, but not always the best method to use.

While fiberglass structural failures, like separating hull/deck joints or cracked hulls, do occur, they are rare. More common are problems with the more complex secondary systems of propulsion, plumbing and wiring. Leaks at ports and deck fittings are not unusual in older boats, but if the vessel was designed and built properly, those will be easy to fix.

Any surface where hardware is mounted outside must be bolted to a backing plate of metal or plywood inside to distribute the stresses. Some of the best builders drill and tap stainless steel backing plates to take the machine screws from fittings. Screws alone are not adequate for any load-bearing deck hardware.

Look for a hull/deck joint that is bolted together (not screwed or riveted) and secured with a permanent polyurethane adhesive or fiberglass laminate.

Materials

Most boats sold before the 1980s were built with orthophthalic resins, which are inexpensive, flexible and moderately waterproof. Today, most builders laminate their hulls with the superior (and more expensive) isophthalic resins, but the top companies also use vinylester resins in the layers closest to the surface gel coat. Vinylester is expensive, but it is the least permeable of all the polyester resins; only epoxy is less permeable and epoxy has other drawbacks.

Good construction today calls for a high-quality gel coat, applied in three passes of about six mils thickness in each pass. Then, a layer of chopped glass fully saturated in vinylester resin makes a secure barrier to water. After that, each hull and deck will have a specific schedule of glass cloth and mat set in isophthalic resin, perhaps with a coring material of end-grain balsa, PVC foam or plywood.

Over 80 percent of the boats built today are built with blended resins, not pure isophthalics or vinylesters. This produces lower emissions in building and a nice looking surface, but experts debate the effect of blended resins on a boat's life span. One says flatly that the force behind boatbuilding now is low atmospheric emissions, not strength or longevity.

Some surveyors believe that boats today are not built any better than they were 10-20 years ago. Ortho- and iso-resins have a higher elongation to failure (are more stretchy) than vinylesters, thus good early laminates were long-lived. Some engineers believe that the mismatch of modern stiff resins and flexible glass will cause problems in the future for boats built in the '90s.

Surveys

Buying a boat is not quite like any other purchase. Houses are simple and their construction is widely understood. Cars are complex but are produced in such quantities that any flaws are well publicized. Boats are customized so that each one is full of individual quirks and they are complicated enough that it takes an expert to separate the good from the bad. That expert is a marine surveyor.

One surveyor I know asks her Monday morning callers, "What did you fall in lust with over the weekend?" Marrying the wrong boat will carry many of the same penalties as marrying the wrong person. The surveyor's job is to inject a healthy dose of reality into the relationship.

The Cruising Sailor by Tom Dove

Surveyors inspect boats for several reasons and you must let him or her know why you want a particular job done. Sometimes it's to check on the quality of repairs after extensive work, other times to inform a lender if a vessel is solid enough to be collateral for a loan. When you buy a boat, you want to know if the boat is sound and suitable for the use you have in mind. You want to be certain you are getting what you think you are paying for. It is good to know a boat's frailties, even if they are not extensive enough to reject the purchase.

The Pre-survey

You can make preliminary judgments yourself. Certainly, you know how large and expensive a vessel you want, approximately what sort of interior layout will work best for you and whether the boat's lines are appealing. You probably have preferences in cockpit and deck layout, power plant or sail rig and perhaps hull shape. You may prefer certain builders to others.

If the boat is small or inexpensive, you may not need to hire a surveyor at all. It makes little sense to pay hundreds for a professional opinion of a $2000 vessel with no engine, electrical system or plumbing. I believe any boat costing five figures calls for a pro unless you have considerable expertise and even a knowledgeable skipper should get a survey before buying a $50,000 boat.

After seeing a number of factories, I would also have an independent survey of a new boat. I know of a 40-footer from a well-known builder that burned as a result of bad wiring at the factory and of new hulls from popular companies that have failed in use. It is especially important to be sure the builder has followed good marine practice to prevent fire or explosion.

You can sort out truly bad boats with a careful inspection. Plumbing and electrical systems can be replaced and engines can be rebuilt if they are not too far gone, but a rotten hull or deck is a peril forever.

Walk across the deck and listen. Does it give way underfoot or emit crackling sounds? That's delamination, a fatal flaw that will take much time and money to fix. Reject the boat. Examine the underwater area of the hull. Is it covered with blisters? That's an expensive repair, requiring removal of the gel coat and reconstruction of the surface layers. A few scattered, shallow blisters are not a problem, but walk away from a boat that has serious blistering unless you can negotiate a dramatic price reduction that will compensate your cost and hassle of repairs.

Look at the underbody for signs of weeping that indicate saturation of the laminate or core, especially in the rudder. A saturated rudder isn't a firm "don't buy" sign, but you will need to have it repaired. Waterlogged rudders are fairly common in older boats. Grab the rudder and pull it back and forth to check for play in the shaft; do the same with the propeller but remember this is somebody else's boat and don't be too aggressive. If either moves noticeably in its bearings, you are looking at a repair job.

Check a sailboat's rigging and any lifelines for failure by wiping the wires with a Kleenex while wearing gloves to protect your hands. Any snags will catch the tissue; snags indicate broken strands and a wire that should be replaced. Also look closely at the fittings with a magnifier to see if any tiny cracks are visible. A cracked fitting will fail sooner or later. Rigging work isn't cheap and insurance will not usually cover a failure that is the result of corrosion or fatigue.

Take up the floorboards, open cabinets, lift cushions and gaze deep into the boat's innards. Shine a bright light into every place you can, squeeze into the tight spaces on hands and knees and look, look, look. Look for rusty drive shafts and keel bolts, for deteriorated wiring and plumbing. A well-kept boat should not have a filthy bilge or scruffy-looking engine, which are symptoms of neglect and will impair the surveyor during a thorough inspection.

The Cruising Sailor by Tom Dove

Look behind the electrical panel if you can (don't disassemble somebody else's boat), checking for neatness, lack of corrosion, and evidence of overheating like melted wire insulation or scorching at connections. The batteries should not have a lot of wires running from them. Every circuit should connect to a circuit breaker at the panel. Rewiring is expensive and any wiring more than about 15 years old is suspect -- especially if a Saturday morning engineer has been modifying it.

If the boat passes these preliminary checks and meets your other requirements, you might make an offer to buy it, subject to a satisfactory report from an independent marine surveyor. Satisfactory to whom? To you, the buyer. Don't let anybody else define it.

Finding a Surveyor

The first rule is to find a surveyor yourself, not through the owner or broker selling the boat. However, I successfully broke the rule when we bought CRESCENDO in 1980 by asking the broker to recommend a surveyor. He gave me a list and I chose one who did a first-rate job. Buying a good boat is easy when you find a broker you can trust. Marine professionals develop reputations that are well known throughout this small community.

Many excellent surveyors are not accredited by any independent agency, so ask for references and check them. If you have no other leads inside the industry, contact the National Association of Marine Surveyors or Society of Accredited Marine Surveyors for a list, but don't rely on these memberships alone. The American Boat and Yacht Council does not accredit surveyors.

What the Surveyor Does

The Cruising Sailor by Tom Dove

A complete survey requires hauling the boat out of the water for inspection of its underbody. Boatyards can schedule a quick haul out so the surveyor can study the boat as it hangs in the Travelift slings.

John P. Kaufman
Figure 19

Sailboat being brought out of the water by a Travelift.

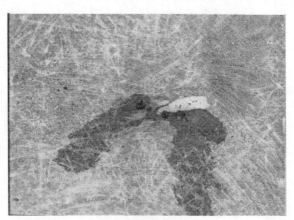

John P. Kaufman
Figure 20

This photo shows the gel coat has been removed from

The Cruising Sailor by Tom Dove

the bottom, allowing a bottom blister to weep. This blister was only one of many on the boat, requiring repair.

The inspection continues with sounding the entire hull and deck to locate voids in the laminate, which are potential sources of failure. Surveyors generally use a lightweight plastic hammer or a screwdriver handle to tap the hull, listening for hollow spaces. Next, the surveyor will use a moisture meter to check for water saturation of the hull; interpreting the readings is not simple, so do not try to do this yourself.

After that comes a thorough inspection of the interior of the hull, the condition of the rigging, wiring, plumbing and an analysis of the boat's general condition. It should include finding potentially troublesome features such as difficult engine or shaft access, improper mounting of deck hardware, badly supported mast and stays, poor grade materials or inadequate structural reinforcement.

Some surveyors perform engine tests, but many do not. Unless you have a good understanding of engines, hire a mechanic to inspect and report on the power plant, especially in a large vessel. If the electrical system is complex, you may need to call in a qualified marine electrician for a close look. The average marine surveyor is a general practitioner, not a specialist.

I favor surveyors who are intimately familiar with the standards of the American Boat and Yacht Council, although this organization does not address construction scantlings, concentrating instead on systems. If your chosen person shows up at the marina with a couple of thick ABYC volumes, be thankful.

The cost depends on the type and size of the boat. Typical rates for purchase surveys start around $12 per foot of boat length for typical cruising craft (1999, Chesapeake Bay), not including yard fees for haul out, bottom cleaning or other preliminary work. Travel is extra, so it pays to find a good surveyor in the vicinity of the boat.

What You Get

The surveyor prepares a written report, describing the boat and the type of service it is designed for. The report also contains a description of the basic construction, any flaws discovered, condition of the various installed systems, known problems common to other boats of the same kind and a recommendation for usage limits. You shouldn't take a boat designed for protected lakes across an ocean, for example. The length and quality of the written report varies widely from one surveyor to another, so you should ask to see a sample of a surveyor's work before starting the job.

You are paying for knowledge. Remember the story of the man who hired George Washington to survey his land, then objected to the $100 cost and demanded an itemized bill. Washington then sent him a bill listing two items:

Stakes $1

Knowing where to put stakes $99

Chapter 9
The Cruising Spectrum

No other sport I know encompasses such breadth as the spectrum of sailing. You can sail in childhood, adulthood and old age, in perfect health or in infirmity. You can spend practically nothing, or you can pour a fortune into it. You may get your thrills from sailing a dinghy on a gusty lake or a sturdy little ship on the largest ocean.

Even the band of that spectrum which we call cruising holds a rainbow of choices. The greatest beauty of it is that no one type of cruising is better than another. They are simply different.

The week-ender need not feel inferior to the ocean voyager, nor the summertime coastal cruiser to the liveaboard family. We all choose the niche which fits our lifestyle, with the knowledge that if our desires change, so can our boats.

While some skippers begin with small week-enders and progress through larger vessels to a big cruiser, many others start right in the middle of the size range or even at the top. Some sailors buy one boat and keep it the rest of their lives, while others trade as regularly as commuters change automobiles. Some build or buy a boat and set off across an ocean, while others take pleasure in gunkholing along the coast.

They are all right, because there's no one, best way to cruise. Cruising may be the last realm where we can make totally independent choices in life and achieve success or failure entirely according to our own efforts. Space may be the final frontier for massive governments or industries; cruising is it for the rest of us.

This is what makes cruising in a sailboat the perfect teaching tool for children. It will reinforce the lessons of the classroom and add many of its own, including the value of family teamwork and the need to respect Nature.

You don't have to cruise full-time to realize these benefits. You can have the benefits of life ashore, including the pleasures of work, a stable community life, integration of your family with relatives, the joy of nice possessions, the intrigue of technology, access to a wide range of cultural events and a broad-based, modern education for your kids by simply adding cruising to your activities.

Pam and I chose to teach, both for the satisfaction of doing something that might alter lives and for the two-month summer vacation that allowed us to go sailing. We liked our suburban house, our little luxuries, our friends and neighbors, the fine schools for our kids and being able to care for our aging parents. I'd say we chose something like the typical American way and it is good.

Some of our friends have concentrated on business success, retiring early or creating sabbaticals that let them own large sailboats and cruise the world. Others have sold their houses ashore and moved aboard to explore the world. I think all these approaches are equally valid.

I admire the skill of those who can build their own vessels and set sail in them, but anything finer than chopping a two-by-four is beyond my ability. I'll take another job I enjoy and hire a skilled carpenter to do such work on my boat. The finances work out about the same, as long as the home-builder counts the value of his time.

I deeply respect the seamanship of couples who sail across the Atlantic or around the world, but will put my boat onto the deck of a freighter if I want to get it to the Mediterranean, thank you. We have put our cruising experience into

The Cruising Sailor by Tom Dove

action with low risk by chartering in Europe and the Caribbean instead of taking CRESCENDO there. If your excitement threshold is higher than mine, you will make other decisions.

As a cruising sailor you have many choices and any one of them will enrich the life you have now.

We all are granted some combination of time, money and health and that allocation changes constantly. If your finances call for a small, older boat, get one. If your time only allows two weeks and a few weekends a year, take them now and figure out how to increase them in the future. If your physical condition requires boat modifications, have them made.

Learning to cruise on a sailboat is not rocket science and buying a boat does not require a fortune. You have the time somewhere in your life and a fascinating world is out there. What are you waiting for?

The Cruising Sailor by Tom Dove

Appendix One
Boat Design Formulas

The easiest way to use these formulas is to plug them into a computer spreadsheet, but a scientific calculator can do the job.

1. Displacement/Length Ratio (use 2,240 pound long tons for Displacement here. Metric tons of 1,000 kg are close enough)

$$D/L = \text{Displacement} / (LWL / 100)^3$$

2. Sail Area/Displacement Ratio (standard is 100 percent foretriangle area, not genoa jib area).

$$SA/D = \text{Sail Area} / (\text{Displacement in pounds} / 64)^{0.66}$$

3. Limiting Displacement Hull Speed.

Speed limit = 1.34 x Square root of the LWL

4. Ballast/Displacement Ratio.

$$B/D = \text{Ballast in pounds} / \text{Displacement in pounds}$$

5. U.S. Sailing Capsize Screening Value Beam in feet.

Screening Value = Beam in feet / (displacement in pounds / 64)$^{0.33}$

6. Ted Brewer's Comfort Value

Comfort Value = Displacement in pounds / (0.7 x LWL + 0.3 x LOA) x 0.65 x (Beam)$^{1.33}$

7. Roll Time Calculation.

You can judge a boat's stiffness by its roll time; a stiff boat will have a quick roll. Get the boat rocking as hard as possible from side to side (you may need helpers to do this) in calm water and record the number of seconds it takes for ten complete rolls, gunwale to gunwale and back. Divide this number by ten to get the average time per roll and then multiply that by the maximum beam, in feet.
Using this method, a heavy cruiser with a high D/L ratio should yield a number from about 2.9 to 3.1, a medium D/L cruiser about 2.6 to 2.8, and a light displacement racer about 2.3 to 2.5.
Stiff boats resist heeling (leaning over when the wind blows hard) but often have a less comfortable motion than more tender vessels, which heel easily.

Appendix Two
Sources

American Boat and Yacht Council - 3069 Solomons Island Road, Edgewater MD 21037. (410) 956-1050. www.abycinc.org. They can answer many questions about boat standards and surveying.
BOAT/US - 880 S. Pickett Street, Alexandria VA 22304. (703) 823-9550. www.boatus.com. Lobbies government for boating, promotes safety, sells equipment at discount in stores and by catalog, brokers insurance, publishes an interesting newsletter. It's worth joining their nonprofit safety foundation.
Chesapeake Bay Magazine - 1819 Bay Ridge Avenue, Annapolis MD 21403. (410) 263-2662. Strictly the Chesapeake, balanced about 2/3 power to 1/3 sail and strong on local knowledge as well as general interest boating articles.
Cruising World Magazine - 5 John Clarke Rd., Box 3400, Newport RI 02840-0992. (800) 727-8473. Originally an ocean voyaging magazine, now expanded to include chartering, coastal cruising and even a bit of racing.
Defender Industries - 42 Great Neck Road, Waterford CT 06385. (800) 628-8225. www.defenderus.com. Big discount marine supply house has the most extensive catalog of all. You should have it, at least to negotiate prices with other stores and find phone numbers of

The Cruising Sailor by Tom Dove

many manufacturers. Retail store in NYC area.

Fawcett Boat Supply - 110 Compromise Street, Annapolis MD 21404. (410) 267-8681 Gets my vote for the best chandlery on the East Coast. Salespeople are knowledgeable and will order anything not in their extensive inventory. Discounts are available, even on books. No electronics.

Good Old Boat - 7340 Niagara Ln. N, Maple Grove MN 55311-2655. (612) 420-8923. www.goodoldboat.com. This new magazine shows great promise, specializing in older boats and the people who love them. Lots of good project articles. Six issues per year, subscription only, no advertising.

Latitude 38 - 15 Locust Ave, Mill Valley CA 94941. (415) 383-8200. Every sailor's favorite West Coast sailing publication. It's breezy and informative.

Marine Associates, Inc. - 3 Church Circle, Suite 232, Annapolis MD 21401. (410) 626-8545. email: sbcanfield @aol.com. Susan Canfield has an excellent short written summary of "How to prepare for a marine survey."

Messing About In Boats - 29 Burley St., Wenham MA 01984-1943. (978) 774-0906. I love this homespun rag. Strictly little boats, mostly homebuilt, mostly wood. Great adventure ideas for anybody who liked "The Wind in the Willows." 24 issues per year, subscription only.

Multihulls Magazine - 421 Hancock St., North Quincy MA 02171. (800) 333-6858. If catamarans and trimarans interest you at all, this is the magazine you need.

National Association of Marine Surveyors - P.O. Box 9306, Chesapeake VA 23321. 800-822-6267. www.namsurveyors.org. Members are accredited as NAMS-CMS (Certified Marine Surveyor).

National Ocean Service (NOS) - For orders: Distribution Division, NOS, 6501 Lafayette Avenue, Riverdale MD 20737-1199. (301) 436-6990. Agency of the National

The Cruising Sailor by Tom Dove

Oceanographic and Atmospheric Administration (NOAA) which surveys and publishes charts and tide tables.

Practical Sailor - 14 Regatta Way, Portsmouth RI 02871. (800) 829-9087. The title is the greatest oxymoron in boating, but this newsletter is solid and interesting, with no commercial strings hampering its test reports. 20 issues per year, subscription only, no advertising.

SAIL Magazine - 84 State Street, 9th Floor, Boston MA 02109-2202. The largest circulation of any sailing magazine in the world, covering all aspects of the sport, with articles for all levels of skill and experience.

SAILING Magazine - 125 E. Main St. P.O. Box 249, Port Washington WI 53074. (414) 284-3494. www.sailnet.com/sailing. Known for its tabloid format and excellent, large photos. Some good articles, too.

Society of Accredited Marine Surveyors - 4162 Oxford Avenue, Jacksonville FL 32210. (800) 344-9077. www.marinesurvey.org. Members are accredited as SAMS-AMS (Accredited Marine Surveyor).

Soundings - 35 Pratt Street, Essex CT 06426. (860)767-3200. www.soundingspub.com. A tabloid newspaper, regionalized to reflect the interests of specific areas. Excellent classified section makes it a good place to shop for a used boat.

Spinsheet - 301 Fourth Street, Annapolis MD 21403. (410) 216-9309. www.spinsheet.com. The East Coast version of Latitude 38, with plenty of local color from the Chesapeake.

US Sailing - PO Box 1260, 15 Maritime Drive, Portsmouth RI 02871-0907. (888) US SAIL-6. www.ussailing.org. Formerly United States Yacht Racing Union until somebody decided that sounded too snobbish. The premier sail racing organization, it also has good publications and lots of technical information useful to cruis-

The Cruising Sailor by Tom Dove

ers.

West Marine - Catalog Sales Division, P.O. Box 50050, Watsonville CA 95077-5050. (800) 262-8464. www.westmarine.com. Oodles of nationwide stores, often in small waterfront towns, with discount boat supplies. Their catalog is a good reference and salespeople are often helpful and knowledgeable (the company hires many liveaboard cruisers).

Woodenboat Magazine - PO Box 78, Naskeag Road, Brooklin, ME 04616 USA. (800)-877-5284. www.woodenboat.com. A wooden vessel isn't the logical choice for a newcomer to cruising, but this beautiful, well-written magazine makes you want one, anyway.

Yachting Magazine - 20 E. Elm St., Greenwich CT 06830. (203) 625-4480. www.yachtingnet.com. This venerable publication currently emphasizes large vessels, especially motor yachts.

Appendix Three
Tools & Supplies

This list has been compiled through the joint effort of our staff and many contributing writers.

As you delve deeper into boating, you will always find a need for one more tool, or a few more supplies. It is truly a case of "Too much is never enough and enough is always too much." With this in mind it is best to adapt the following to your boat's needs and storage capacity.

The boat tools should not be shared with the car or the home. Purchase a good quality plastic tool box larger than the current need. Remove the handle which will certainly come off when you are transferring the box to the boat or the dock. A second box for less used tools is also a good idea.

* Tools for a small cruising sailboat without electrical or plumbing systems.

** Tools to add to the list for a mid-sized cruiser with electrical, plumbing, electronics and an inboard engine.

*** Tools for the long-term cruiser or liveaboard sailor intending to make most of the repairs to most of the systems.

The balance of the list will be needed at your land base for extensive repairs, renovations, upgrades and restoration projects.

The Cruising Sailor by Tom Dove

Hand Tools

Good brands will carry a life time warranty.
* # 1, #2, #3 Phillips screwdrivers.
* Thin blade 3/16", medium blade 1/4", heavy blade 3/8" straight screwdrivers.
All the above should also be purchased in the stubby length.
** Jewelers set of screwdrivers.
** Various square drivers if you have this type of fastener on your boat. You will have to know the sizes you will need.
* Linesman pliers.
** Dikes/side cutters.
** Wire strippers. Buy the type with the stripper portion before the hinge.
** Terminal crimps.
** Digital multi-meter.
* Long-nose pliers.
** Needle-nose pliers.
* Vise Grips
* Small slip joint pliers (opens to 2").
*** Straight blade sheet metal cutters.
** Caulk gun.
*** Lufkin folding rule with brass slide extension.
** Large and small metal files.
* Set of allen wrenches 1/16" to 7/16" minimum.
*** China bristles paint brushes with an angle cut, in sizes 1", 1-1/2", 2", 2-1/2".
** School pencils.
** Pencil sharpener.
** Thin blade awl.
* 8" & 12" adjustable wrench.
** 12" Lenox hacksaw with 18, 24, & 32 teeth per inch blades.
** Estwing leather handle straight claw hammer.

The Cruising Sailor by Tom Dove

*** A #2, & #3 nail set.
** Combination wrench set.
** 1/4" drive socket set.
* 3/8" drive socket set.
** Ignition wrench set.
The term "set" is used because most of these tools are sold in sets. You can purchase them individually but you will spend more than buying a set.
** 24" to 36" adjustable wrench. The size will depend on the prop nut size of your boat.
** Battery carrying strap.
** Feeler gauges (blade type).
** Cordless drill with two batteries, charger, cobalt drill bits ranging from 1/32" to 3/8" and screwdriver bits with a good holder. These should be the same size as your hand screwdrivers.
** Large slip joint pliers (opens to 4").
*** 2# Ballpeen hammer.
Caulking iron.
*** Rubber mallet.
*** Small & large Wonder bars.
*** Diston small dovetail saw.
*** Diston coping saw.
*** Diston 13 point hand saw.
*** Stanley 25' tape measure.
*** Stanley combination square.
*** Stanley #40 wood chisels 1/2", 3/4", 1".
These are the only Stanley tools you should own.
*** Block plane.
*** Half round wood file/rasp.
*** Heavy blade awl.
*** Larger size drill bits 7/16" to 1" forsener bits are the best for large wood bits. Metal bits should be cobalt.
*** Brad point bits 1/16" to 3/8".
Plug cutters 3/8" to 3/4"
*** Hole saw set.

*** Metal chisel and drift set.
** Right angle-straight and Phillips screwdrivers.
** Fish tape.
** Heavy gauge terminal crimp tool.
** Line wrench set.
** 1/2" drive socket set.
** Deep well socket set for all the different size drives you now own. Some of these may have been included when you purchased the sets.
*** 1/2" Breaker bar.
*** 1/2" Click stop torque wrench.
** 1/2" drive large sockets for all the bolts/nuts which are larger than the sets contain.
** Wrenches for the same bolts/nuts.

Power Tools

Purchase brand name, heavy duty, commercial grade tools with a high ampere draw. These are the only tools that will last.
3/8" & 1/2" power drills.
Circular saw with good carbide tooth blades.
*** Random orbiting sander with 5" & 6" pads. Buy your 3M gold sanding disk in the 6" size and cut them down when you need the 5" size. Buy rolls of these grits. 60, 80, 100, 120, 150, 180.
Power miter box with an 80 tooth carbide blade.
3" x 24" or 4" x 24" belt sander. Buy at least three belts of each of these grits. 36, 80, 100, 120.
*** Soldering gun with electrical solder and flux.
Heat gun.
*** Random orbit buffer if you own a fiberglass boat.
Scrolling jigsaw with various wood and metal blades.
Router with various bits purchased as the jobs warrant. Always use roller bearing bits where applicable.
*** Sawz-all with various size and types of blades for

The Cruising Sailor by Tom Dove

wood/metal.
Biscuit jointer with at least two hundred of the two larger size biscuits.
*** 25', 50', & 75' #12 wire extension cords.
Table or radial arm saw. The radial arm saw can be set up with a multitude of attachments to handle many different functions other than cross cutting and ripping.

Supplies
All Stainless Steel Fasteners

** At least 50 each of these Phillips head screws.
#4 x 1/2", 3/4", 1" Flat and oval head.
#6 x 1/2", 3/4", 1", 1-1/4", 1-1/2", 1-3/4", 2" Flat and oval head.
#8, #10, #12 Same as #6 plus 2-1/2", 3" Flat and oval head.
** Finish washers for each of the above size screw numbers.
#6, #8, #10, 1/2", 3/4", 1", 1-1/2" Pan head.
** At least 10 each of these fasteners.
1/4" x 20 x 2", 3", 4" Flat and stove head bolts with 2 washers and 1 nut each.
5/16" & 3/8" x 1", 1-1/2", 2", 2-1/2", 3" machine bolts with 2 washers and 1 nut each.
** Cap nuts for each of the above sizes.
*** 1/4" x 2", 3", 4", 5" lag bolts with washers.
** Large fender washers for each of the above sizes.
*** 2 pieces of solid rod 3' long in 1/4", 3/8", 1/2".
*** 2 pieces of threaded rod 3' long with 6 nuts and washers per piece in 1/4", 3/8", 1/2".
* Various size cotter pins to replace ones which will need to be removed. Check the sizes you need before ordering or purchase a cotter pin kit with various sizes included.
18 gauge brass or stainless steel brads in 1/2", 3/4", 1"

Electrical

** Butt terminals, male and female quick disconnect terminals. Order at least 50 each for wire gauges, 22-18, 16-14, 12-10, 8.
** Spade connectors, stud connectors. Order at least 50 each for the same gauge of wire above to fit around stud sizes 4-6, 8-10, 1/4", 5/16", 3/8".
*** 10 terminals for each size battery cable in use on your boat.
** 6 battery clamps (lugs, the kind used on your car) with stud. Do not connect the battery wires directly to the clamp; use the stud and terminals.
** 200 each of 6" & 11" medium duty wire ties.
*** 100 each of 3/4" and 1-1/2" cable clamps.
*** 1 each 4, 6, 8, 10 position terminal blocks. 6 each 20 amp in-line fuse holders with 5 each of, 5 amp, 10 amp, 15 amp, & 20 amp fuses.
*** 100 ft each of wire gauges 18, 16, 14, 12, 10, 8. Tinned marine primary wire.
*** 25 ft each of wire gauges 6 & 4.
*** 10 butt connectors for 6 & 4 wire.
*** 10 ft of battery cable for each size you have in use on board.
*** 2 ft each of heat shrink tubing 3/16", 1/4", 3/8", 1/2," 3/4".

Misc. Electrical Supplies

** Liquid electrical tape.
** Vinyl electrical tape.
** Nylon string to use as a wire fishing device.
** 1 Pair of battery jumper cables. They must be long enough to reach between the banks of batteries you may need to jump. If you can not find them this long, make up your own with heavy ends and # 2 battery cable.
** Jumper wires for testing. These can be made with 4 alligator clips and 12 gauge wire.

The Cruising Sailor by Tom Dove

** 1 breaker or fuse holder for each different size and type you on have board.
** 1 fuse for each specialty fuse on board.
** 1 switch for each type on board.
** 2 extra bulbs for each type on board.
** 1 lamp socket for each type on board.
*** 1 of each shore line end or an extra 50' shore line set.
** 1 connector for each type of electronic instrument connector on board.

Sealants, Paint and Repair Products

** 1 tube each of Teak Deck Systems, 3M 5200 in white, GE silicone in white & clear, Star Bright polysulfide underwater sealant, Sea Repair.
** 1 small kit each of Epoxy, Marine Tex, Boat Yard fiberglass with 6 oz. cloth and matching gel coat colors.
*** 1 qt each of varnish, top sides paint for each color on board, stain, paint thinner, acetone, lacquer thinner, Penatrol, boiled linseed oil.
*** Coffee cans.
*** Plastic pots in 1 qt size.
*** Disposable brushes in 1/2", 1", 1-1/2", 2", 2-1/2".

Plumbing Parts

* The best method of determining your needs for plumbing will be to go through your supply and waste systems measuring each hose, clamp, tubing and fitting type and size. With this list in hand purchase at least two of each type of fitting, 10 of each size clamp, hose to replace the longest length of each size or fittings and hose to patch in the very long lengths. As with your shore power line, carry an extra water supply hose of no less than 50'. Also purchase water hose repair ends.

** This may not be considered plumbing by some, but it carries water, therefore it is included in this section. Your engines have many small sizes and lengths of hoses. As with the plumbing hoses, buy enough to replace the longest length of each size with the proper size clamps. These should be the heavy wall hose with wire reinforcement.

** If you have large exhaust lines you do not need to carry a full length. Do carry a large coffee can with 4 hose clamps which are a larger size than the exhaust hose. You must carry at least one spare impeller or a rebuilding kit with the impeller included for every pump on board. THIS IS A MUST!

Misc. Supplies

* Shock cords and ends.
* Buckets.
* Sponges.
* Chamois.
** Toilet brush.
** Scrub brush.
** Deck brush with handle.
*** Roller handle, pan and pads.
** Bronze wool.
** Bronze scrub brush.
** Detergents.
** Cleaning products.
** Polishes.
** Compounds.
** Water resistant/proof glue.
*** Extension cord ends.
** Patching material for every inflatable on board.
** Repair parts for engine(s).
*** Antifreeze.
** Oils.
** Grease gun with grease.

The Cruising Sailor by Tom Dove

** Transmission fluid.
* 5 gals of extra fuel.
* Duct tape.
* Riggers tape.
*** Masking tape.
*** Sheet sand paper in grits 50, 80, 100, 120, 150, 180, 220. At least 5 sheets of each grit.
* At least two complete sets of dock lines and anchor rodes.
* One 3/4" line (regardless of boat size to 45') three times the length of the boat. (Tow line)

The Cruising Sailor by Tom Dove

Glossary

This glossary has been compiled through a joint effort of the staff of Bristol Fashion Publications and many writers. It is not intended to cover the many thousands of words and terms contained in the language exclusive to boating. The longer you are around boats and boaters the more of this second language you will learn.

A

Accumulator Tank-A tank used to add air pressure to the fresh water system thus reducing water pump run time.
Aft-Near the stern.
Amidships-Midway between the bow and stern.
Antifouling-Bottom paint used to prevent growth on the bottom of boats.
Arrangement Plan-The drawing that shows the berths, galley and head inside the hull.
Athwartships-Any line running at a right angle to the fore/aft centerline of the boat.

B

Backer Plate-Metal plate used to increase the strength of a through-bolt application, such as with the installation of a cleat.
Ballast-Weight added to improve sea handling abilities of the

boat or to counterbalance an unevenly loaded boat.
Beam-The width of the boat at its widest point.
Bilge-The lowest point inside a boat.
Bilge Pump-Underwater water pump used to remove water from the bilge.
Binnacle-A box or stand used to hold the compass.
Body Plan-The drawing showing the shape of the hull in an athwartships plane. Also called Sections.
Bolt-Any fastener with any head style and machine thread shank.
Boot Stripe-Trim paint of a contrasting color located just above the bottom paint on the hull sides.
Breaker-Replaces a fuse to interrupt power on a given electrical circuit when that circuit becomes overloaded or shorted.
Bridge-The steering station of a boat.
Brightwork-Polished metal or varnished wood aboard a boat.
Bristol Fashion-The highest standard of condition any vessel can obtain and the highest state of crew seamanship. The publishing company which brought you this book.
Bulkhead-A wall running across (athwartships) the boat.
Butt connectors-A type of crimp connector used to join two wires end to end in a continuing run of the wire.

C

Canvas-A general term used to describe cloth material used for boat coverings of any type. A type of cloth material.
Carlin-A structural beam joining the inboard ends of deck beams that are cut short around a mast or hatch.
Cavitation-Reduced propeller efficiency due to vapor pockets in areas of low pressure on the blades. Turbulence caused by prop rotation which reduces the efficiency of the prop.
Centerboard-A hinged board or plate at the bottom of a sailboat of shallow draft. It reduces leeway under sail.

The Cruising Sailor by Tom Dove

Center of Effort-(CE) The geometric center of the total sail plan on a sailboat. Used to determine lee or weather helm.

Chafing Gear-Any material used to prevent the abrasion of another material.

Chain-Equally sized inter-looping oblong rings commonly used for anchor rode.

Chain Locker-A forward area of the vessel used for chain storage.

Chine-The intersection of the hull side with the hull bottom, usually in a moderate speed to fast hull. Sailboats and displacement speed powerboats usually have a round bilge and do not have a chine. Also, the turn of the hull below the waterline on each side of the boat. A sailboat hull, displacement hull and semi-displacement hull all have a round chine. Planing hulls all have a hard (sharp corner) chine.

Chock-A metal fitting used in mooring or rigging to control the turn of the lines.

Cleat-A device used to secure a line aboard a vessel or on a dock.

Clevis-A Y-shaped piece of sailboat hardware about two to four inches long that connects a wire rope rigging terminal to one end of a turnbuckle.

Coaming-A barrier around the cockpit of a vessel to prevent water from washing into the cockpit.

Cockpit-Usually refers to the steering area of a sailboat or the fishing area of a sport fishing boat. The sole of this area is always lower than the deck.

Companionway-An entrance into a boat or a stairway from one level of a boat's interior to another.

Construction Plan-A drawing showing all the parts that make up the hull structure. The plan and profile are drawn.

Cribbing-Large blocks of wood used to support the boat's hull during it's time on land.

Cutless Bearing®-A rubber tube that is sized to a propeller

shaft and which fits inside the propeller shaft strut.

D

Davit-Generally used to describe a lifting device for a dinghy.

Deadrise-The angle that a hull bottom makes with the horizontal. Measured in the aft part of the hull but more commonly at the stern. If the stern is flat from port to starboard, it has zero deadrise.

Deck Camber-An arbitrary curve that the deck has from port to starboard.

Deck Plan-A drawing showing all the structure and hardware on the deck.

Delaminate-A term used to describe two or more layers of any adhered material that have separated from each other due to moisture or air pockets in the laminate.

Device-A term used in conjunction with electrical systems. Generally used to describe lights, switches receptacles, etc.

Dinghy-Small boat used as a tender to the mother ship.

Displacement-The amount of water, in weight, displaced by the boat when floating.

Displacement Hull - A hull that has a wave crest at bow and stern and which settles in the wave trough in the middle. A boat supported by its own ability to float while underway.

Dock-Any land-based structure used for mooring a boat.

Down Flooding-When water enters an open hatch or ladder.

Draft-The distance from the waterline to the keel bottom. The amount of space (water) a boat needs between its waterline and the bottom of the body of water. When a boat's draft is greater than the water depth, you are aground.

Dry Rot-This is not a true term as the decay of wood actually occurs in moist conditions.

F

Fairing-The process of smoothing a portion of the boat so it will present a very even and smooth surface after the finish is applied.

Fairing Compound-The material used to achieve the fairing process.

Fairlead-A portion of rigging used to turn a line, cable or chain to increase the radius of the turn and thereby reduce friction.

Fall-The portion of a block-and-tackle system that moves up or down.

Fastening-Generally used to describe a means by which the planking is attached to the structure of the boat. Also used to describe screws, rivets, bolts, nails etc. (fastener)

Fiberglass-Cloth like material made from glass fibers and used with resin and hardener to increase the resin strength.

Filter-Any device used to filter impurities from any liquid or air.

Fin Keel-A recent type of keel design. Resembles an up-side-down T when viewed from fore or aft.

Flame Arrestor-A safety device placed on top of a gasoline carburetor to stop the flame flash of a backfiring engine.

Flat Head-A screw head style which can be made flush with or recessed into the wood surface.

Float Switch-An electrical switch commonly used to automatically control the on-off of a bilge pump. When this device is used, the pump is considered to be an automatic bilge pump.

Flying Bridge-A steering station high above the deck level of the boat.

Fore-The front of a boat.

Fore-and-Aft-A line running parallel to the keel. The keel runs

fore-and-aft.
Forecastle-The area below decks in the forward most section of the boat. (pronunciation is often fo'c's'le)
Foredeck-The front deck of a boat.
Forward-Any position in front of amidships.
Freeboard-The distance on the hull from the waterline to the deck level.
Full Keel-A keel design with heavy lead ballast and deep draft. This keel runs from the stem, to the stern at the rudder.

G

Galley-The kitchen of a boat.
Gel Coat-A hard, shiny coat over a fiberglass laminate which keeps water from the structural laminate.
Gimbals-A method of supporting anything which must remain level regardless of the boat's attitude.
Grommet-A ring pressed into a piece of cloth through which a line can be run.
Gross Tonnage-The total interior space of a boat.
Ground Tackle-Refers to the anchor, chain, line and connections as one unit.

H

Hanging Locker-A closet with a rod for hanging clothes.
Hatch-A opening with a lid which opens in an upward direction.
Hauling-Removing the boat from the water. The act of pulling on a line or rode is also called hauling.
Hawsehole-A hull opening for mooring lines or anchor rodes.
Hawsepipes-A pipe through the hull, for mooring or anchor rodes.
Head-The toilet on a boat. Also refers to the entire area of the bathroom on a boat.
Helm-The steering station and steering gear.

Holding Tank-Used to hold waste for disposal ashore.
Hose-Any flexible tube capable of carrying a liquid.
Hull-The structure of a vessel not including any component other than the shell.
Hull lines-The drawing of the hull shape in plan, profile and sections (body plan).

I

Inboard-Positioned towards the center of the boat. An engine mounted inside the boat.
Inboard Profile-A drawing of the centerline profile of a boat showing the interior arrangement on one side.

K

Keel-A downward protrusion running fore-and-aft on the center line of any boat's bottom. It is the main structural member of a boat.
King Plank-The plank on the center line of a wooden laid deck.
Knees-A structural member reinforcing and connecting two other structural members. Also, two or more vertical beams at the bow of a tugboat used to push barges.

L

Launch-To put a boat in the water.
Lazarette-A storage compartment in the stern of a boat.
Lead-The material used for ballast. Also, pronounced "leed," (as in leading a horse) when denoting the distance separating CE and CLP in a sail plan. (See above)
Limber holes-Holes in the bilge timbers of a boat to allow water to run to the lowest part of the bilge where it can be pumped out.
LOA-Length Over All. The overall length of a boat.
Locker-A storage area.

Log-A tube or cylinder through which a shaft or rudder stock runs from the inside of the boat to the outside of the boat. The log will have a packing gland (stuffing box) on the inside of the boat. Speed log is used to measure distance traveled. A book used to keep record of the events on board a boat.

LWL-Length On The Waterline. The length of a boat at the waterline.

M

Manifold-A group of valves connected by piping to tanks. They allow filling and removal from one or more tanks.

Marine Gear-The term used for a boat's transmission.

Mast-An upward pointing timber used as the sail's main support. Also used on power and sail boats to mount flags, antennas and lights.

Metacenter-A graphically determined point in stability calculations at one angle of heel.

Mile-A statute mile (land mile) is 5280 feet. A nautical mile (water mile) or knot is 6080.2 feet.

Mizzen Mast-The aftermost mast on a sailboat.

Mold Loft-A floor where hull lines are drawn full size. Patterns for construction are taken from the mold loft.

N

Nautical Mile-A distance of 6080.2 feet.

Navigation Lights-Lights required to be in operation while underway at night. The lighting pattern varies with the type, size and use of the vessel.

Nut-A threaded six-sided device used in conjunction with a bolt.

Nylon-A material used for lines when some give is desirable. Hard nylon is used for some plumbing and rigging fittings.

O

Outboard Profile-A drawing of the outside of a hull. Sometimes called a styling drawing.

Oval Head-A screw head design used when the head can only be partially recessed. The raised (oval) portion of the head will remain above the surface.

Overhangs-The length from the bow or stern ending of the waterline to the forward or aft end of the hull.

P

Painter-A line used to tow or secure a small boat or dinghy.

Panel-A term used to describe the main electrical distribution point, usually containing the breakers or fuses.

Pan Head-A screw head design with a flat surface, used when the head will remain completely above the surface.

Pier-Same general usage as a dock.

Pile-A concrete or wooden post driven or otherwise embedded into the water's bottom.

Piling-A multiple structure of piles.

Pipe-A rigid, thick-walled tube.

Planing Hull-A hull design, which under sufficient speed, will rise above it's dead in the water position and seem to ride on the water.

Planking-The covering members of a wooden structure.

Plug-A term used to describe a pipe, tubing or hose fitting. Describes any device used to stop water from entering the boat through the hull. A cylindrical piece of wood placed in a screw hole to hide the head of the screw.

Port-A land area for landing a boat. The left side of the boat when facing forward.

Propeller (Prop, Wheel, Screw)-Located at the end of the shaft. The prop must have at least two blades and propels the vessel through the water with a screwing motion.

R

Radar-An electronic instrument which can be used to see objects as blips on a display screen.

Rail-A non structural, safety member, on deck used as a banister to help prevent falling overboard.

Reduction Gear-The gear inside the transmission housing that reduces the engine Rpm to a propeller shaft Rpm that is optimum for that particular hull and engine.

Ribs-Another term for frames. The planking is fastened to these structural members.

Rigging-Generally refers to any item placed on the boat after the delivery of the vessel from the manufacturer. Also refers to all the wire rope, line, blocks, falls and other hardware needed for sail control.

Righting Arm-A term used in stability calculations. The distance between the center of gravity of a hull and the center of buoyancy at one particular angle of heel.

Ring Terminals-A crimp connector with a ring which can have a screw placed inside the ring for a secure connection.

Rode-Anchor line or chain.

Rope-Is a term which refers to cordage and this term is only used on land. When any piece of cordage is on board a boat it is referred to as line or one of its more designating descriptions.

Round Head-A screw or bolt head design with a round surface which remains completely above the material being fastened.

Rudder-Located directly behind the prop and is used to control the steering of the boat.

Rudder Stock-Also known as rudder post. A piece of round, solid metal attached to the rudder at one end and the steering quadrant at the other.

S

Samson Post-A large piece of material extending from the keel upward through the deck and is used to secure lines for mooring or anchoring.
Screw-A threaded fastener. A term for propeller.
Screw Thread-A loosely spaced course thread used for wood and sheet metal screws.
Sea Cock-A valve used to control the flow of water from the sea to the device it is supplying.
Sections-Also, Body Plan. The shape of a hull in an athwartships plane, that is perpendicular to the waterline.
Shackle-A metal link with a pin to close the opening. Commonly used to secure the anchor to the rode.
Shaft-A solid metal cylinder which runs from the marine gear to the prop. The prop is mounted on the end of the shaft.
Shear Pin-A small metal pin which is inserted through the shaft and the propeller on small boats. If the prop hits a hard object the shear pin will shear without causing severe damage to the shaft.
Sheaves-The rolling wheel in a pulley.
Sheet Metal Screw-Any fastener which has a fully threaded shank of wood screw threads.
Ship-Any seagoing vessel. To ship an item on a boat means to bring it aboard.
Shock Cord-An elastic line used to dampen the shock stress of a load.
Single Sideband Radio (SSB)-A high frequency (HF) radio system used for long-range communications.
Slip-A docking space for a boat. A berth.
Sole-The cabin and cockpit floor.
Spade Rudder-A rudder that is not supported at its bottom.
Stability-The ability of a hull to return to level trim after being

heeled by the forces of wind or water.
Stanchion-A metal post which holds the lifelines or railing along the deck's edge.
Starboard-The right side of the boat when facing forward.
Statute Mile-A land mile which is 5280 feet.
Stem-The forward most structural member of the hull.
Step-The base of the mast where the mast is let into the keel or mounted on the keel in a plate assembly.
Stern-The back of the boat.
Strut-A metal supporting device for the shaft.
Stuffing Box-The interior end of the log where packing is inserted to prevent water intrusion from the shaft or rudder stock.
Surveyor-A person who inspects the boat for integrity and safety.
Switch-Any device, except breakers, which interrupt the flow of electrical current to a usage device.

T

Tachometer-An instrument used to count the revolutions of anything turning, usually the engine, marine gear or shaft.
Tack Rag-A rag with a sticky surface used to remove dust before applying a finish to any surface.
Tank-Any container of size that holds a liquid.
Tapered Plug-A wooden dowel tapered to a blunt point and is inserted into a seacock or hole in the hull in an emergency.
Tender-A term used to describe a small boat (dinghy) used to travel between shore and the mother ship.
Terminal Lugs-Car style, battery cable ends.
Through Hull (Thru Hull)-Any fitting between the sea and the boat which goes through the hull material.
Tinned Wire-Stranded copper wire with a tin additive to prevent corrosion.
Topsides-Refers to being on deck. The part of the boat above

the waterline.
Torque (or Torsion)-The rotating force on a shaft. (lb-in)
Transmission-Refers to a marine or reduction gear.
Transom-The flat part of the stern.
Trim-The attitude with which the vessel floats or moves through the water.
Trip Line-A small line made fast to the crown of the anchor. When weighing anchor, this line is pulled to back the anchor out and thus releases the anchor's hold in the bottom.
Tubing-A thin-walled cylinder of metal or plastic, similar to pipe but having thinner walls.
Turnbuckles-In England they are called bottle screws. They secure the wire rope rigging to the hull and are used to adjust the tension in the wire rope.
Turn of the Bilge-A term used to refer to the corner of the hull where the vertical hull sides meet the horizontal hull bottom.

V

Valves-Any device which controls the flow of a liquid.
Vessel-A boat or ship.
VHF radio-The electronic radio used for short range (10 to 20-mile maximum range) communications between shore and vessels, and between vessels.

W

Wake-The movement of water as a result of a vessel's movement through the water.
Washer-A flat, round piece of metal with a hole in the center. A washer is used to increase the holding power of a bolt and nut by distributing the stress over a larger area.
Water Pump-Any device used to pump water.
Waterline-The line created at the intersection of the vessel's

hull and the water's surface. A horizontal plane through a hull that defines the shape on the hull lines. The actual waterline or just waterline, is the height at which the boat floats. If weight is added to the boat, it floats at a deeper waterline.

Web Frame-The transverse structural members (frames) in a boat hull, installed port to starboard. Longitudinal frames are installed fore and aft.

Weight list-A compilation of every item in the boat. A calculation is made of the weight and center of gravity of everything on board. This is the only way a designer can estimate the displacement of the boat.

Wheel-Another term for prop or the steering wheel of the boat.

Whipping-Refers to any method used, except a knot, to prevent a line end from unraveling.

Winch-A device used to pull in or let out line or rode. It is used to decrease the physical exertion needed to do the same task by hand.

Windlass-A type of winch used strictly with anchor rode.

Woodscrew-A fastener with only two thirds of the shank threaded with a screw thread.

Y

Yacht-A term used to describe a pleasure boat of some size. Usually used to impress someone.

Yard-A place where boats are stored and repaired.

Z

Zebra Mussel-A small freshwater mussel which will clog anything in a short period of time.

The Cruising Sailor by Tom Dove

INDEX

ABYC	47, 89, 97
Aft cabins	17, 67
Anchor	
designs	69, 70, 77, 78
hand signals when setting	61
mishaps	63, 64
rodes	70-72
techniques	61, 72
Ballast/Displacement	95
Beam	16, 17, 55, 56, 58
C&D Canal	40
CRESCENDO	34, 54, 58, 70, 87
Cal 34	45
Calculations	
Comfort	58, 96
Sail power	52, 95
Size	49, 95
Speed	53, 95
Stability	56, 96
Worldwide Web sites with	59
Camper cruising	20
Capsize Screening Value	57, 96
Catalina	15, 20, 58
Catamarans	55, 56, 57, 62, 67
Center cockpits	67
Chesapeake Bay	17, 40, 45, 47, 63, 66, 67

Page 125

Comfort Committee	41
Comfort Value	58, 96
Construction	
materials	50, 83-84
of fiberglass laminates	79-82
of hull/deck joint	82-83
quality	47, 81-83
techniques	80-82
Cooking	21, 22, 47
Cutter	27, 32-33
Delaware Bay	40
Dickerson 37	66
Dinghy	
Mishaps	23-24, 64
Small boat	53
Displacement/Length ratio	49-52, 95
Docking	
at fuel docks	73-74
in slips	75-76
using spring line	74, 75
Draft	
Air (overhead)	18
Water	17
Electrical	
panels	47, 87
wiring	47, 82, 87
Engine	
inboard	48
outboard	20
Ensign	20
Fiberglass	
cloth and resin	79
cores	80
layup	79-82
molds for	79, 80
"pan" liners	82

parts bonding	83
structural failure	83
Florida Keys	21-24
Freeboard	29
Furling	34
Gelcoat	81, 84
Halyards	
for jib with roller furling	34
led to cockpit	34
Head compartment	
on small boat	20
on midsize boat	45, 79
Hull form	27
Icebox improvement	47
Keel shape	30-32
Ketch	33, 36, 67
Length	
LOA	15
LOD	16
LWL	16
Length/beam ratio	55
Long Island Sound	40, 44
Maine	18, 56, 61
Morgan 34	45
Navigation	
bearings	43
by GPS	43, 61, 66
charts	21, 61, 66
fix	43
Line of Position	43
New Jersey coast	39
Nova Scotia	61
O'Day	20
Power	
changing jibs to control	33
from sail area	52

related to SA/D ratio	52
related to wind strength	53
Radar	61
Rainbow	20
Resin	
blended	84
epoxy	83
isophthalic	83
orthophthalic	83
vinylester	83
Sabre 34	45
Safety	
grabrails for	45, 46
footing for	45, 46
jacklines for	39
at night	42, 61
Sail Area/Displacement	52, 95
Schooner	33, 36
Sleeping accomodations	
large boat	67
leecloths	42
midsize boat	42
quarter berth	42
settees	42
small boat	21
vee berths	21, 42
Sloop	20, 32, 39, 63, 67
Sparkman & Stephens	20
Speed	
and planing	53, 54
average offshore	53, 55
displacement limitations on	53
of multihulls	51, 55
weight related to	51
Spinnaker, cruising	34, 45, 66
Stability	

    and heeling 55-57, 96
    from ballast 17, 56
    from beam 16, 56
    Range of Positive 57
    Screening Value 57, 96
    tender vs stiff 56, 58
    Ultimate 57
Survey
    ABYC standards in 87, 89
    cost 89
    for purchase 85
    for insurance 85
    finding a surveyor 87, 97
    of new boats 85
    Pre-survey 85
    reports 90
    surveyor certification 87
Tanzer 20
Tartan 30 45
Venture/Macgregor 20
Watches 42, 61
Waves 17, 29, 40, 51-53, 55, 58
Weather
    Chesapeake squall 64
    Florida cold front 21
Weight
    and displacement 49
    and power 51
    and waves 51
    effect on motion 58
Wind against current 40
Yawl 33, 37

Books published by Bristol Fashion Publications
Free catalog, phone 1-800-478-7147

Boat Repair Made Easy — Haul Out
Written By John P. Kaufman

Boat Repair Made Easy — Finishes
Written By John P. Kaufman

Boat Repair Made Easy — Systems
Written By John P. Kaufman

Boat Repair Made Easy — Engines
Written By John P. Kaufman

Standard Ship's Log
Designed By John P. Kaufman

Large Ship's Log
Designed By John P. Kaufman

Custom Ship's Log
Designed By John P. Kaufman

Designing Power & Sail
Written By Arthur Edmunds

Fiberglass Boat Survey
Written By Arthur Edmunds

Building A Fiberglass Boat
Written By Arthur Edmunds

The Cruising Sailor by Tom Dove

Buying A Great Boat
Written By Arthur Edmunds

Outfitting & Organizing Your Boat For A Day, A Week or A Lifetime
Written By Michael L. Frankel

Boater's Book of Nautical Terms
Written By David S. Yetman

Modern Boatworks
Written By David S. Yetman

Practical Seamanship
Written By David S. Yetman

Practical Seamanship
Written By David S. Yetman

Captain Jack's Basic Navigation
Written By Jack I. Davis

Captain Jack's Celestial Navigation
Written By Jack I. Davis

Captain Jack's Complete Navigation
Written By Jack I. Davis

Southwinds Gourmet
Written By Susan Garrett Mason

The Cruising Sailor
Written By Tom Dove

Building A Fiberglass Boat
Written By Arthur Edmunds

The Cruising Sailor by Tom Dove

Daddy & I Go Boating
Written By Ken Kreisler

My Grandpa Is A Tugboat Captain
Written By Ken Kreisler

Billy The Oysterman
Written By Ken Kreisler

Creating Comfort Afloat
Written By Janet Groene

Living Aboard
Written By Janet Groene

Simple Boat Projects
Written By Donald Boone

Racing The Ice To Cape Horn
Written By Frank Guernsey & Cy Zoerner

Boater's Checklist
Written By Clay Kelley

Florida Through The Islands
What Boaters Need To Know
Written By Captain Clay Kelley & Marybeth

Marine Weather Forecasting
Written By J. Frank Brumbaugh

Basic Boat Maintenance
Written By J. Frank Brumbaugh

Complete Guide To Gasoline Marine Engines
Written By John Fleming

The Cruising Sailor by Tom Dove

Complete Guide To Outboard Engines
Written By John Fleming

Complete Guide To Diesel Marine Engines
Written By John Fleming

Trouble Shooting Gasoline Marine Engines
Written By John Fleming

Trailer Boats
Written By Alex Zidock

Skipper's Handbook
Written By Robert S. Grossman

Wake Up & Water Ski
Written By Kimberly P. Robinson

White Squall - The Last Voyage Of Albatross
Written By Richard E. Langford

Cruising South
What to Expect Along The ICW
Written By Joan Healy

Electronics Aboard
Written By Stephen Fishman

A Whale At the Port Quarter
A Treasure Chest of Sea Stories
Written By Charles Gnaegy

Five Against The Sea
A True Story of Courage & Survival
Written By Ron Arias

The Cruising Sailor by Tom Dove

Scuttlebutt
Seafaring History & Lore
Written By Captain John Guest USCG Ret.